The Preacher's Library
Volume 1

Why Preach?

CW00550009

Peter Dawson

ISBN 1 85852 172 6

INTRODUCTION

Preaching is a very particular form of communication which has always been important in the life of the Christian Church. At the beginning of the twenty-first century we are undergoing a revolution in the varieties, method and speed of our communications. Preachers of all denominations, ordained and lay, undertake this calling with an awareness that we preach in a changing context.

The Preacher's Library is designed to help us think through, perhaps in some cases reassess, why we preach, how we preach, and to whom we preach. Some of the volumes in this series will take a fresh look at familiar issues, such as how preachers should approach various parts of the Bible, how we understand and express our doctrinal inheritance and the variety of styles in which preaching can be done. Other volumes will introduce issues which may be less familiar to many of us, such as the significance of our cultural context or the way in which the self-understanding of a woman preacher has important things to say to all preachers. Some of these books will offer direct help in the practice of preaching. Others will deal with issues which, although they appear more theoretical, impinge upon the preacher's task and on which we therefore need to have reflected if we are to preach with integrity in today's world.

All the writers in this series, lay and ordained, women and men, are recognised preachers within their own denominations and write with the needs of their colleagues firmly in mind. These books will avoid academic jargon, but they will not avoid dealing with difficult issues. They are offered to other preachers in the belief that as we deepen our thinking and hone our skills

God's people will be blessed and built up to the glory of God.

In *Why Preach?* Peter Dawson faces the negative connotations the word has in many people's minds. Even within the Christian church there is much uncertainty about whether its long and distinguished history as part of worship and as a means of communication still has contemporary validity. He writes from the conviction that preaching is not a means of sharing information about God, it is a means of creating the possibility of an encounter *with* God. As such, it is the means by which God's presence has been realised in the past, and will be realised in the new millennium.

This book is not intended to be an objective and scholarly account of homiletical theories. Rather, it offers a highly personal view of how one person sees the nature and purpose of preaching. Mr Dawson's sometimes unfashionable views, often vigorously expressed, will not command universal agreement. But love it or hate it, this book offers a huge challenge to preachers of all persuasions to pursue their calling with conviction.

Michael J Townsend

CONTENTS

The next best thing to good preaching is bad preaching. I have more thoughts while enduring it than at other times.

Ralph Waldo Emerson 1863

1

WHY PREACH?

O n Easter Day 1627, one of the greatest preachers the church has ever known offered this pearl of wisdom in a sermon at St Paul's Cathedral:

> There is nothing that God has established in a
> constant course of nature, and which therefore
> is done every day, but would seem a miracle,
> and exercise our admiration, if it were done
> but once.[1]

John Donne went on to give the sunrise as an example. If it happened only once, our amazement would have no end. 'Only the daily doing,' he said, 'takes off the admiration.'

Donne was leading his congregation towards a consideration of the miracle of the Resurrection. But what he had to say as his sermon began might have been a homily about the very nature of preaching itself. Many people have been powerfully affected by one fine sermon, but regular doses of sermonising have dulled their senses and taken off the admiration. After two thousand years of sermons, is anyone listening?

After conducting a wedding, I was addressed at the church door by a very elderly gentleman who said, 'That were a fine wedding, vicar. Tell me, do you do funerals?' I didn't like to inquire why he was asking. But that incident illustrates how, in the matter of conducting a service, one thing can lead to another. Ideally, every time the word of God is offered, it should lead those present to want to come again and hear more. This book attempts to explore how that purpose may be achieved.

Today, the very word preach is dyslogistic: it is used to indicate disapproval. That is reflected in one of the meanings of the verb 'preach' given in the *Oxford English Dictionary*: 'To give moral or religious advice in an obtrusive or tiresome way.' One sometimes gets the impression that the greatest sin someone leading worship can commit is to give a long sermon. Kenneth Hulbert, the surgeon son of a distinguished Methodist, used frequently to observe of a certain preacher that he passed some good stopping places.

Although it has brought other benefits, the emergence of all-age worship has done little for those who wish to preserve the pre-eminence of the sermon. A youth leader observed to me: 'We don't want sermons here. We are trying to encourage the young people to come to church.' No longer are young Christians to be encouraged to understand and respond to preaching as a regular feature of worship. If they are to be attracted to and remain within the life of the church, say some, sermons must go.

Youth rallies, such as those organised so splendidly by the Methodist Association of Youth Clubs, do not address this problem. Rather, they exacerbate it. After the mind-blowing, soul-searching, spirit-lifting experience of power preaching at a MAYC rally, young people return to their churches to experience the greatest let-down since the *Titanic* hit an iceberg. One of the greatest failures of the church in the twentieth century has been its surrender to the popular notion that it is futile to expect young people to sit down and listen. They are thirsting to hear the gospel preached with power in a language relevant to their needs, anxieties and fears. When it is done well, they are spellbound.

The task of the preacher today is made harder than before because authority in all its forms is under attack.

Invited during my time as a headmaster to write a piece for a local paper on my educational priorities, I wrote that young people needed to be taught to respect their parents, obey their teachers and keep the law. The editor rang me up to thank me. 'That,' he said, 'is just the sort of controversial stuff I was hoping for.'

The controversy Jesus caused when he first began to preach is powerfully described in the opening chapter of Mark's gospel. In the synagogue at Capernaum, the people were astonished at what they heard, saying to one another: 'He speaks with authority.' There are many preachers today who, week by week, speak with authority from the nation's pulpits. It is my contention that we should follow their example rather than look for some new way of passing on the gospel that eliminates the sermon as a vehicle for making known God's will and offering salvation. There has been laughter in hell as the church has steadily demoted the preacher's role.

Scripture is the foundation of the preacher's message, although there are as many ways of building on it as there are preachers. Keeping in mind the scriptural hard core under one's feet is essential if the message is to stand the test of time and circumstance. The pulpit is not a place to speculate on which political party Jesus would have voted for, or whether he who made the earth and sky favours European union, or which economic policy will most quickly bring in the kingdom of God. Yes, of course Christianity has political and economic implications, but at its peril does the church hitch its preaching of the gospel to one generation's version of what is politically correct.

The preacher lives in a state of constant tension. While expounding the implications of the gospel may mean supporting changes in social values, it may just as readily mean demanding a return to past standards. So the preacher must resist two temptations. The first is to go along with whatever version of morality happens to be in fashion simply because it *is* fashionable, and accepting it will make the church appear relevant. The second is to be everlastingly demanding a return to the good old days when all questions of right and wrong might be settled in a trice by reference to simple and straightforward rules the implications of which remain beyond dispute. Permanently to adopt one or other of these positions is an abdication of responsibility.

The preacher's task is surely to guide his or her hearers between the Scylla of fashionableness and the Charybdis of worshipping the past. In one of his fictitious tales of Lake Wobegon, a small town in Minnesota untouched by time, Garrison Keillor describes the people's attitude to religion: 'We go in for strict truth and let the other guy be tolerant of us.'² Sometimes that sentiment seems to be in the minds of Christian folk both sides of the liberal/conservative divide, does it not? We all surrender to the temptation from time to time.

Avoiding dependence on the simplicities of old-time religion does not mean that the preacher is free of a duty to challenge the even greater simplicities of the do-as-you-like society. But it takes courage in the present day, as it did in the days of the Old Testament prophets, to speak up against godlessness and moral laxity. 'You cannot be serious!' raged John McEnroe when a tennis umpire failed to share his view of which side of the line the ball had fallen. The same response often greets those who dare to challenge the hedonistic nature of Western society today. It is part of the preacher's destiny to live with the you-cannot-be serious response.

In its preaching, the readiness of the church to adapt its position to match contemporary thinking on religious, social and moral issues, and to claim that it is being prophetic in doing so, leaves many worshippers confused. It has not succeeded in attracting new worshippers by its commitment to relevance and abandonment of moral imperatives. Preachers' general reluctance to shock the world into asking, 'What shall we do?' is notable. Perhaps Abraham Lincoln had something when he said, 'When I hear a man preach, I like to see him act as if he were fighting bees.'

That is not to suggest stirring people up by being outrageous serves any purpose. There is a kind of preaching which appears to be based simply on generating fury and bewilderment in hearers. The excuse given for this is that it shakes people out of their complacency. That's like a pilot ensuring his passengers pay attention to the pre-flight explanation of how to wear a safety harness by warning them there is almost sure to be a crash. The likely outcome is that passengers will choose to get off the aircraft, which is what happens when a preacher sets out to outrage a congregation.

George Bernard Shaw once observed that all the young can do for the old is shock them. Preachers in their twenties, along with some who wish they still were, are sometimes more Shaw than sure in their approach. Any preacher whose method is predominantly that of lobbing theological, sociological or political grenades will merely create a wasteland. But raising the hackles of one's hearers is a perfectly proper preaching device if the occasion calls for it. The experiences of Saint Paul and John Wesley illustrate the point.

Paul catalogues for us (2 Corinthians 11:24-25) the various forms of maltreatment his preaching had brought upon him: 'Five times I have received from the Jews the forty lashes minus one. Three times I was beaten with rods. Once I received a stoning.' John Wesley's treatment by hostile elements in the crowds he addressed out of doors is well recorded in his journal. Being pelted with mud was a common occurrence. At Bradford in Wiltshire he had opposition so memorable that he made a joke about it:

> The beasts of the people were tolerably quiet until I had nearly finished my sermon. They then lifted up their voices, especially one, called a gentleman, who had filled his pocket with rotten eggs. But a young man, coming unawares, clapped his hand one each side and smashed them all at once. In an instant he was perfume all over, though it was not so sweet as balsam.[3]

While it would be overstating the case to suggest that today's preachers would benefit from a taste of the rotten egg treatment, the desire to be a popular preacher is all too common. Seeking the adulation of the media, and first prize in a national preaching contest, seem to the present writer contrary to the very spirit and purpose of delivering the gospel message.

There has always been an inclination for worshippers to prefer some preachers to others. It is a feature which emerged very early in the church's history. We find clear evidence of it in the first and third chapters of Paul's first letter to the church in Corinth, where we read of the Christians dividing themselves according to their allegiance to different preachers, and quarrelling among themselves as a result.

My part in advising sixth-formers about university entrance once took me to the University of Keele, where undergraduates wishing to study arts subjects had to follow a course in science as well, and vice versa. Knowing the apprehension with which my historians regarded subjects like physics, I was interested to learn in advance of my visit to Keele that the most popular science subject among arts specialists was astronomy. All became clear when I attended a lecture by the astronomy professor. Tall and elegant, with flowing waves in his golden hair, his mellifluous tones fell like honey on the listeners' ears. His eloquent exposition of a knowledge of astronomy as essential to the future was dazzling. He could have sold central heating systems in the Sahara and had little difficulty in selling astronomy, especially to female undergraduates.

Was it the professor or his message that was most powerful? It was impossible to say. That is the way with preachers as well as academics trying to encourage commitment to their subjects. The medium and the message are one. In the life of the church, that raises a critical problem which Paul clearly identified, and which is still with us today. It is simply expressed: 'If our faith depends upon the eloquence of the preacher, where does that leave us?'

Eloquence is a beguiling skill that may mislead those subject to it, and indeed those in possession of it. Not that Paul was opposed to mastery of declaring the gospel with all the eloquence at a preacher's command. He had no quarrel with Apollos, a rising star in the preaching firmament whom some Corinthians loved to hear. He saw him as a man building effectively on the foundation he himself had laid:

> According to the grace of God given to me, like a skilled master builder I laid a foundation, and someone else is building on it. Each builder must choose with care how to build on it. For no one can lay any foundation other than the one that has been laid; that foundation is Jesus Christ.
>
> 1 Corinthians 3:10-11

Paul goes on to challenge those who might wish to build on the foundation of the gospel message using gold or silver. He will have no truck with giving golden phrases priority over the simple gospel, or the silver tongue precedence over the salvation message.

All preachers fall into this trap. How easy it is to choose a story to tell from the pulpit just because it is a good story, not minding too much whether it actually fits the gospel teaching we claim to be spelling out. So, there are preachers who turn the sermon into a music hall turn, or a party political broadcast, or a wind-up about protecting the Amazonian rain forests. But they build in vain whose sermons are not founded on Jesus Christ.

Except in the very general sense of wanting to spread the gospel and realise the presence of God, the immediate purpose of a sermon varies, most obviously according to the listeners being addressed. A good illustration of that is provided by the contrast between Peter's great sermon in Jerusalem at Pentecost (Acts 2) and the way in which

Paul addressed the Athenians (Acts 17). The outcome in each case also provides an interesting dissimilarity. 'What should we do?' said the people in Jerusalem whom Peter had cut to the heart. 'We will hear you again about this,' said those of a philosophical turn of mind in Athens, to whom Paul had skilfully quoted one of their own favourite poets, Epimenides of Crete (Acts 17:28).

These illustrations from the life of the early church are reminders to all preachers to have regard to those who will hear what has been prepared. They teach us that carting a particular sermon around from one congregation to the next is an abdication of responsibility. If part of the answer posed at the beginning of this chapter – why preach? – is to supply spiritual food according to people's needs, the preacher must recognise that not everyone is on the same diet. The mature Christian needs something stronger than the simple gospel that brought him or her to the Lord; a congregation made up largely of young professionals and business executives making their way in the world must be spoken to differently from the ladies' bright hour; preaching in an inner city mission requires a different approach from doing so in a rural chapel. If all that seems to be a statement of the obvious, experience suggests that it is not at all so for some preachers.

A Methodist local preacher once told me, 'My message is always about the power of the Holy Spirit.' He never preached about anything else. This relieved him of the need to spend long hours in preparation, but failed to serve the needs of his hearers. Before any preacher starts preparing a sermon, he or she should sit down and think about the people to whom it will be offered. That is not easy for local preachers as they will probably visit a particular congregation only a few times a year and never get to know its members closely. Ministers responsible for several churches may have a similar problem.

A consideration of what the Methodist Church expects of its ministers tells us a good deal about how it perceives the role of the preacher. The service for the ordination of presbyters in the *Methodist Worship Book* (1999) contains the following definition of their role:

> . . . to preach by word and deed the Gospel of God's grace; to declare the forgiveness of sins to all who are penitent; to baptise, to confirm and to preside at the celebration of the sacrament of Christ's body and blood; to lead God's people in worship, prayer and service; to minister Christ's love and compassion; to serve others . . .

While not significantly different from the definition in the *Methodist Service Book* (1975), that reveals a noticeable change from what appeared in Methodism's *Book of Offices* (1936):

> You are chosen and elect to be evangelists of the grace of God in Christ Jesus, sent forth to make disciples of all nations; to teach and to premonish, to feed and provide for the household of God; to seek for Christ's sheep that are dispersed abroad, and for whom He laid down His life, and for the children of God who are in the midst of this world, that they may be saved through Christ forever.

That which followed was at the heart of Methodist theology at the time the *Book of Offices* was written. The end purpose of the minister's role was spelled out:

> Wherefore consider with yourselves the end of your ministry; and see that you never cease your labour, your prayer and diligence, until you have done all that lieth in you, according to your bounden duty, to bring all such that are committed to your charge unto that true conversion of heart and life through personal trust in Christ alone . . .

Nothing could more clearly demonstrate the perception of Methodist preaching that applied at the time. The notion of conversion through a personal relationship with Jesus, so much at the heart of the Methodist message in the 1930s, was of its time. In continental Europe, a different kind of messiah was emerging from the wilderness.

In January 1933, Adolf Hitler had become German chancellor. The following month, Hermann Goering, one of Hitler's earliest followers, established the *geheime statspolizei*, the secret state police force which became known as the *gestapo*. The establishment of the Hitler Youth movement followed. By 1934 boys were raising their right hands in the Hitler salute and swearing an oath of allegiance:

> I consecrate my life to Hitler;
> I am ready to sacrifice my life for Hitler;
> I am ready to die for Hitler, the saviour,
>   the führer.[4]

In his book *Hitler's Table Talk*, the historian Hugh Trevor-Roper records the führer as having this to say to his rapt listeners at dinner one day:

> It is between the ages of ten and seventeen that youth exhibits both the greatest enthusiasm and the greatest idealism. It is for this period of their lives that we must provide them with the best possible instructors and leaders. For once youth has been won over to an idea, an action like that of yeast sets in.[5]

The truth of those words is not diminished by the subsequent actions of the man who spoke them. For good or evil, the young, and the not-so-young, will follow those they admire. As those ready to follow Hitler grew in number, and the German war machine increased in strength, in Britain a nervous and unstable coalition government under Neville Chamberlain pursued a policy of appeasement.

Between 1935 and 1938, with awesome timeliness, the great historian H A L Fisher published the three volumes of his magnificent *History of Europe*, in which he analysed the rise of European civilisation from its earliest origins with the Greeks. In the preface, he warned that he could discern no plot or rhythm in Europe's development, only 'one emergency following another, as wave upon wave'. Fisher added that all he could recognise in the development of human destinies was the play of the contingent and unforeseen. He asked whether, in face of the rise of totalitarianism, peace would be preserved and freedom survive. Would Europe, and the world beyond, be saved from tyranny?[6]

It was against the background of fearsome events that the Methodist Church formulated the *Book of Offices*, in which the task of its ministers was defined. Not without good cause did Methodism look back to the Wesleyan doctrine of personal salvation and call upon its ordinands to bring men and women to a true conversion of heart and life through personal trust in Christ, and Christ alone.

If the contrast between Methodism's current perception of the role of a minister and its position in the 1930s is stark, no less is true of the difference between its definition of the local preacher's role when the *Methodist Service Book* was introduced in 1975 and the position now. At the end of the third quarter of the twentieth century, the requirements laid on a local preacher at the time of commissioning were, apart from insistence on preaching nothing at variance with Methodist doctrine, mostly to do with attending meetings as laid down in standing orders. Perhaps that was simply a reflection of Methodism's rather quirky preoccupation with maintaining the right organisation and structure, down which road some of its leaders seemed to think salvation lay. Be that as it may, it created the impression that the preaching of someone not ordained was less significant than pulpit utterances made from behind a clerical collar. It is a misconception which is still widely shared. Happily, the new *Methodist Worship Book* introduces a radically revised service for the commissioning of local preachers. Those about to be admitted to the role are told:

> . . . yours is a responsibility rooted in the word
> of God. You will bring salvation to all, in
> season and out of season. As you lead
> worship, your own life will be shaped and
> transformed.

Why preach? Because it is a transforming activity for both preacher and hearer. It is so because there is a third party involved in the preparation and delivery of any sermon, namely the Lord in whose name we presume to enter into the infinitely demanding, endlessly challenging, awesomely life-changing activity we call preaching. Its essential purpose is to evoke the very presence of God. We preach not simply to speak of God's nature as revealed in scripture; not only to make known the implications of that nature for the individual and the world; not merely to help people's faith to grow by examining evidences of God's power. All these elements are fully justified, and others too, but they subserve a mightier purpose: to bring about a life-changing encounter between those to whom we preach and the living God.

Sir Joseph Pope, one time Professor of Mechanical Engineering at Nottingham University, and an expert on metal fatigue, once held an audience spellbound by asking an apparently simple question: 'Why, when hammering a nail into a piece of wood, do we watch the nail, which is stationary, rather than the hammer, which is moving?' The answer is that the human eye, which is fixed on the nail, directs the hammer by way of the body's complex and powerful communications system, which is invisible. 'In the field of engineering science,' said Sir Joseph, 'there is usually a great deal more going on than can be seen.'

A sermon amounts to a great deal more than the words the preacher speaks. The invisible God is at work in the place where they are proclaimed. Paul's insistence (1 Corinthians 2) that the preacher should depend not on his or her own wisdom or eloquence but on the power of the Holy Spirit at work in the preaching situation needs to be taken to heart by all preachers. The only difference between oratory and preaching is that the first is a human activity while the second transcends the human and has its origins, purpose and impact in the divine.

Paul Scott Wilson has written that preaching is the means by which God comes to his people. 'God uses the sermon,' he says, 'for self-revelation.' He quotes Edward Riegert's assertion: 'People are hungry for an encounter with God; they do not merely want to know about God, they want to know God.' At its highest, the words of the preacher become God's words; the preaching place is filled with the presence of the Lord; the promise of God to be with his people is fulfilled.[7]

Peter Barber, the member of the Methodist connexional team with responsibility for local preachers, addressing the question of what should be the focus of preaching, insists that the answer must always be God. Too often, he suggests, worship is issue driven. 'Our commitment to issues,' he says, 'should arise out of our encounter with God.'[8]

The sermon is not the preacher's jaunting-car but God's vehicle. What worshippers hear from the pulpit may go well beyond anything the preacher has actually said. God speaks to his people through the pulpit most intimately, according to their several needs, using the preacher's inadequate words to express himself mightily.

Saint Paul writes of approaching the preacher's task with fear and trembling (1 Corinthians 2:3). Why should we do so? Because the sermon is what Paul Scott Wilson calls 'God's event'.

2

PULPIT PERFORMANCE

The delivery of a sermon is a performance. Those who declaim from the pulpit don't behave like that over their cornflakes at home. Well, most don't. The voices, gestures, mannerisms and style of dress preachers adopt are special to that activity. Some are developed deliberately, others unconsciously. But while a preacher's impact will be in part determined by those aspects of any presentation, what he or she actually says will be the most important factor. That being so, a consideration of different ways of interpreting and expressing the gospel must come first in any analysis of pulpit performance.

In 1995, *The Times* collaborated with the College of Preachers in launching an annual preaching competition. Cassell published twenty of the most successful entries under the somewhat presumptuous title, *The Times Book of Best Sermons*. In her introduction to the book, Ruth Gledhill, the newspaper's religious affairs correspondent, referred to Dr Martyn Lloyd-Jones, who ministered at Westminster Chapel for thirty years until 1968, as 'the last of the great preachers'. She went on to assert that, 'in the comparatively short time that has passed since, preaching has become an increasingly disparaged art'.[1] If the preaching of Lloyd-Jones did indeed mark a high point in the recent history of preaching, following which decline has set in, with no great preachers in evidence, it is worth analysing his pulpit performance.

The writer Christopher Catherwood, grandson of the man known to his Westminster congregation simply as the

Doctor, has written an analysis of his grandfather's preaching in which he asserts that he restored Puritan perspectives to the Christian faith and thereby 'played a key role in bringing back biblical, reformed thinking into evangelical life'. He offers this account of what the Doctor perceived to be the proper basis of preaching:

> Preaching from scripture – biblical exposition – was to him nothing less than God's method. His job as a preacher was not to give his own ideas – London was filled with preachers who did that. Rather he saw his task as making known God's message from God's word. The preacher never spoke with his own authority. Rather, it was an unction from God. This is why he felt that all preaching must be expository – in other words, an exposition by the preacher of what the Bible was saying – because it could never really be anything else if it were to be the genuine article.[2]

The contrast between Martyn Lloyd-Jones' preaching and that of the other great pulpit figures in London in his time was stark. Nearby, at the Methodist Central Hall in Westminster, William Sangster preached on what a religious revival would do to reduce sexual immorality, cut the divorce rate, disinfect the theatre, reduce crime and 'restore to the nation a sense of high destiny'. It was powerful stuff that hit the national newspaper headlines and made clear the relevance of the gospels to the state of the nation.[3] At Kingsway Hall, where Methodists of socialist persuasion worshipped, the fiery Donald Soper related the gospel to current political issues. He it was who, on being asked if it was possible to be a Christian and vote Conservative, replied that it was possible, but he wouldn't advise anyone to put his immortal soul in that kind of danger. At the City Temple, Leslie Weatherhead emphasised the transforming effect of friendship with Jesus on the individual, relating the burgeoning study of human behaviour to the Christian faith in his book, *Psychology in the Service of the Soul.*

The pulpit performance of Martyn Lloyd-Jones was nearer to that of John Calvin. He would take a passage of scripture and examine it verse by verse. For the congregation, it was hard work. Lloyd-Jones had no time for what Catherwood calls man-made thrills. One of the first things he did on arrival at Westminster Chapel was to scrap the choir. Such diversions from the word of God had no place in any service he conducted. People came first and foremost, he believed, to have the meaning of scripture made plain. Any who came for any other reason quickly abandoned this formidably rigorous expositor of God's word, whose character has been described as that of a lion in the pulpit and a lamb in the vestry.

Preachers of all shades of theology and personal belief can, and often do, debate endlessly as to the authority of one perception of preaching compared to another. There were in Martyn Lloyd-Jones' day preachers as great as he whose methods were quite different from his. There are those who would challenge Catherwood's doubtful distinction between using the pulpit to explore the precise meaning of scripture and using it to propound one's own ideas. What is biblical exposition but one person's version of what the Bible means, be it based upon ever so careful a study of a particular passage? The antithesis between preaching scriptural truth and expounding the social and political implications of the gospel is false.

If that be true and, like everything else in this book, it is open to question, what may a preacher learn of performance in the pulpit from Martyn Lloyd-Jones? His own words, in his most famous sermon, 'Joy Unspeakable', on the work of the Holy Spirit, give the answer. Using a technique he frequently deployed, he imagined some in his congregation racing ahead and thinking about what particular gifts they might develop through the power of the Holy Spirit. He said:

> I am sure that many of you will be thinking about that. You wait a minute. I shall deal with the question of gifts when it comes at the right place. You do not start with that. That

comes towards the end of this treatment. But
that is how the devil gets us to bypass the
scriptures in the interests of our particular
point of view.[4]

The message for the preacher is clear. First we must
study scripture and discern its meaning, then we should
decide what to say from the pulpit. But there are many,
are there not, who first decide what they want to say to a
congregation on some matter or other, then look up texts
to support their point of view? It is against such an
approach that the Doctor warns us.

During the thirty years of Martyn Lloyd-Jones'
ministry at Westminster Chapel, familiarity with the Bible
among worshippers, upon which the effectiveness of his
pulpit performance partly depended, was in decline.
Since then, acquaintance with scripture has further
diminished. The findings of a Gallup poll published on
New Year's Eve 1999 showed that fifty-six percent of those
claiming to be Christians could not name the first four
books of the New Testament and that thirty-four percent
could not identify a single one. The analysis suggested
that such ignorance was not entirely limited to nominal
Christians with little or no interest in scripture or
churchgoing.[5]

One reason for people's lack of Bible knowledge has
been the disappearance of the Bible from schools.
Children and young people no longer leave school
familiar with scripture passages. Jesuit teachers say, 'Give
us the child until he is seven and we will show you the
man.' If what we do with our young people in their early
years is powerfully formulative, it is no wonder the rising
generation does not count Bible knowledge very highly,
seeing that their teachers don't. As an Ofsted inspector at
secondary level for most of the 1990s, I have only once
heard the Bible read in a school assembly. In our multifaith and no-faith society, the attention given to the Bible
in religious education in the classroom is slight. As a
result, young people no longer have a treasury of texts in
their minds and hearts to which to turn in their times of

joy and sorrow. Quote a scriptural passage to most people under thirty and they will wonder what you are on about.

The multiplicity of Bible translations has exacerbated the problem and carried it into the churches. There is no longer any common version of scripture known to all, although there was no sign of what was to come when the first significant move to replace the King James Authorised Version of the Bible was made in 1952. The preface to the Revised Standard Version insisted that it was not a new translation in contemporary language but sought to preserve all that was best in the Bible 'as it had been known and used through the years'. But those responsible for subsequent versions have observed no such principle. In a society in which idioms change with astonishing rapidity, rewriting the Bible in contemporary language has become a growth industry.

The journalist Jill Tweedie once observed that the trouble with writing for newspapers is that today's *mot juste* becomes tomorrow's drawer lining. Something of the same might be said of the many idiomatic versions of scripture to appear in the second half of the twentieth century, beginning with the New English Bible in the 1960s. Unsurprisingly, none has proved to be an enduring source of memorable texts. The American author George Ade writes of a music teacher who struggled to teach the piano to one little girl and who, twice a week, tried without success 'to bridge the awful gap between Dorothy and Chopin'.[6] Twice each Sunday, in churches up and down the country, preachers strive to bridge the awful gap between people's acquaintance with the Bible today and the familiarity with biblical texts which men like Martyn Lloyd-Jones were once able to assume.

'Austin Farrer was a giant of a preacher.' So wrote Leslie Houlden, Professor of Theology at King's College, London in 1991, in editing a collection of Farrer's sermons delivered to students in Oxford in the 1950s and 1960s. Warden of Keble College, Farrer was a high Anglican and, as a contemporary of the great non-conformist preachers already described, provides a fascinating comparator.

At a personal level, he came across to me as an austere man; but within a short space of time, wit and humour emerged from behind the scholarly facade. In the pulpit, as in common-room conversation, he was master of the art of using humour to draw in his hearers before taking them into difficult theological territory. Houlden finds something surprising about his popularity as a preacher:

> For one thing, though his sermons often began with an amusing story or striking image, they would flow on into deep waters where not every hearer could easily follow, and their course could be sinuous. Also, they had a literary quality which did not exactly disqualify them as oratory but was certainly becoming unusual in the pulpit of his day (now it has virtually vanished).[7]

Houlden's verdict on Farrer, an academic priest whose complex and sometimes tortuous pulpit presentations made great demands on his hearers, identified him as 'a preacher of his time and place'.

So what has happened since the days when great preachers occupied London pulpits and attracted congregations of between one and two thousand at each service? What has changed since Austin Farrer commanded the pulpits of Oxford? Have we seen, as Ruth Gledhill suggests, and as many people believe, the last of the great preachers? Just as Elijah believed that he was the last of the prophets, have we seen the last of those who preached with power? In order to explore that question, an historical digression is necessary, so let me leave preaching aside for a moment and look at what has happened in society at large since the days of Martyn Lloyd-Jones and his contemporaries.

The 1960s were a watershed in the economic, social and cultural history of the West. As the 1950s drew to a close, economists charted the rise of the consumer society, with increasing affluence bringing new goods and services on the market. On becoming Prime Minister of Britain in

January 1957, Harold Macmillan told the people they had never had it so good.[8] In the same year, Vance Packard published his stunning research into the manipulative strategies being employed to sell the increasing flow of goods and services in the USA and Europe. Called *The Hidden Persuaders*, his book provided a disturbing account of how advertisers were increasingly using the insights of social science and psychiatry to influence people's market decisions.[9] Coincidental with this came a massive increase in the influence of young people in the market. In the 1960s, for the first time, young people began to challenge and to influence what was on offer in shops, in schools, in politics and in places where right and wrong were determined.

In his book *The Sixties*, the historian Arthur Marwick identifies the music of the Beatles, the fashions of Mary Quant and the art of Andy Warhol as illustrating the social trend.[10] Hot pants, the miniskirt and the Lady Chatterley trial challenged traditional moral values. There is a grain of truth in Philip Larkin's famous, perhaps infamous, suggestion that sexual intercourse began in 1963. As Billy Fury took screaming pubescent girls halfway to paradise, the sexual mores of the previous generation were dismissed by increasing numbers of young people.

As their influence increased, young people demanded political and social recognition. In universities across Europe, students marched against the authorities, often led by fiery Marxists who dreamed of establishing a new social order. The rights of adolescents to a voice in the government of the schools they attended were pressed home. In 1971, *Children's Rights* was published, in which liberal educationists such as Leila Berg and Michael Duane argued that children had a basic right to self-determination.[11] In a review, Edward Short, who had been Secretary of State for Education and Science from 1968 to 1970, described the book as 'an impressive onslaught on the savage idiocies with which we, as parents and teachers, indeed as a society, hammer our children into our own image'. In the same year, Penguin published Neil Postman's *Teaching as a Subversive Activity*, suggesting that teachers should become agents of subversion to overthrow the existing educational establishment and equip young people for radical change in society.[12]

As all institutions of authority quaked before the forces of the emergent youth culture, those committed to the old values of discipline and restraint looked on aghast. One such was the young Member of Parliament for Finchley, Margaret Thatcher, who by 1969 was shadowing Ted Short from the opposition benches in the House of Commons. Her election to the Conservative leadership in 1975, and subsequent elevation to become the first woman Prime Minister in 1979, arose at least in part from her being perceived as the apostle of traditional values; the advocate of authority and discipline; the standard-bearer of the old distinctions between right and wrong. But there was not to be, and has not subsequently been, any turning back from the social and moral revolution. The advance of pluralism will continue in the new millennium.

The preacher who would be heard faces the difficult task of holding the balance between the old and the new; of handling the tension between traditional and contemporary morality described in the first chapter. It is a task which makes enormous demands on the preacher's faith, resilience and readiness to discuss almost intolerable points of view in a tolerant way. For example, while many a preacher has grave reservations about the place of active homosexuals in the church, in work with young people generally, and in society at large, surely none would advocate a return to the days when gay men and lesbian women were the victims of persecution. As is so often the case where moral issues are concerned, the key question to which those who listen to preachers want the answer is 'Where do we draw the line?' The fact that different preachers have different answers merely demonstrates that we are all merely searchers after the truth. The only certainty we have is that God loves us, each and every one. In everything else, we see through a glass darkly. In his or her pulpit performance, the preacher equips the congregation to search out, honestly and lovingly, whatever truths God feels its different members might be able to bear in their several pilgrimages of faith. The one thing that is certain is that the God of surprises will surprise us all when we move on from our present struggles and come face to face with the whole truth.

It has, of course, always been the case that people want to go their own way, unrestrained by economic, social, religious or moral conventions. The women who agonised over what their daughters got up to under the influence of Beatlemania in the 1960s had themselves, twenty years before, shrieked and swooned and, as his biographer Arnold Shaw relates, waved their panties at Frank Sinatra in adolescent ecstasy.[13] It is perhaps not without significance that a Sinatra song that has endured throughout the ensuing years has been 'My Way'. Maybe the permissive society began not with the 1960s generation but the one before. As the distinguished social historian George Trevelyan once observed, most great social changes began earlier than we realise. The seeds of the 1960s revolution were planted long before.

The great preaching ministries of the 1950s and 1960s were the product of their time. They were a powerful and passionate call to Christian values in a world that was dying. People were still prepared to gather in great numbers to hear gospel values. It was still permissible, though not as appropriate as once it had been, for someone to assert from the pulpit that Britain was a Christian nation without their being accused of prejudice, or laughed to scorn. Religious education was based on the Bible and churchgoing was still widely practised. None of those features now exists in our society. Their demise has meant the disappearance of the conditions required for great preaching in the sense in which that term was once used.

In the post-Christian era, the old ways of preaching are giving way to new. The overwhelming ability of the media, and especially of television, to empty church pews, has been a further factor in bringing to an end the conditions in which people like Martyn Lloyd-Jones and his contemporaries flourished. Slowly but surely, different ways of preaching have evolved to meet new conditions.

Thomas Macaulay, Member of Parliament for Edinburgh in the middle of the nineteenth century, once famously observed, when addressing the House of Commons, 'The gallery in which the reporters sit has become the fourth estate of the realm.' He was the first fully to appreciate the growing power of the press in the governance of the nation, to match that of the other three estates: the lords spiritual, lords temporal and commons. Along with the press, Macaulay would no doubt have included radio and television in his characterisation, had they been invented.

Few today would question that what the newspapers say shapes the thinking of ordinary people; that what is broadcast on the radio affects their understanding of events; that what appears on television influences their behaviour and very way of life. And the greatest of these determinants of human thought, belief and conduct is television. The power of the glowing pictures in the living room of a home, right at the heart of family life, is enormous. Speaking at the Guildhall in 1965, the author and broadcaster Alistair Cooke had this message for the West about the impact of television on the developing nations:

> People who once knew nothing beyond the horizon are now getting the beginnings of a universal education, but not in any traditional classroom. It is all there, laid out before them for the first time, in a little magic box. You'd be amazed at the silence which can fall on an Asian village or suburb when the evening television programmes begin. Those who watch may have no alphabet, but they know about the good life in Los Angeles. Ignorant they may once have been, but now they discover that what is wrong with their eyes is trachoma and what is wrong with their children is beri-beri. They have long known

that they were sick, but now they know that they are poor, and that it is not written in the stars that it must be so.[14]

The speaker went on to spell out an equally challenging message about the impact of television among the poor and underprivileged in the United States. Sitting in a mean room in a decaying inner city tenement, a man sees the prosperous life of those who have nice houses, clean jobs, and a good education for their children, and realises the extent of his deprivation. 'The media,' said Alistair Cooke, more than thirty years ago, 'have disclosed the rich world to the poor world and acquainted the poor with their own poverty. Ladies and gentlemen, you have been warned.'

There is little in Cooke's entire analysis that would need to be altered if it were to be offered today. The essence of his lecture to the gathering of comfortable middle class professionals and business folk in the affluent context of the Guildhall in 1965 was that television, like the printing press, is an influence for both good and evil. Everything depends on the uses to which the printed word, or the television broadcast, is put. As those now responsible for protecting us from a possible flood of pornography on our television channels struggle to limit the damage, the relevance of his warning increases apace.

One of the major effects of television viewing on the population has been dramatically to reduce people's attention span. Since even the most powerful drama may well be interrupted every now and again by advertisements, enabling viewers to take tea and toast, or beer and burgers, or whatever else takes their fancy, folk are not used to staying with anything for long without a break. Maybe the time has come to have commercial breaks in church. Local shopkeepers might be invited to pop in and tout their wares mid-sermon on Sunday mornings. Such an arrangement would brighten up some services a treat, and offer an additional source of income through profit-sharing. But preachers would have to look to their laurels. It would be sad if, on leaving church, worshippers were heard to observe that they thought the French fries were the best part of the service, much as they say now, after one has slaved over a sermon, 'We liked the hymns.'

While challenges to the importance of preaching should be resisted, today's preachers must offer the gospel to the world as it is rather than ignore what is in effect a fundamental change in how communication takes place. If it is no longer possible for the average preacher to hold a congregation's attention for more than twenty minutes at a time, we must adjust our methodology and techniques to meet that situation. Three considerations provide pointers to the way ahead.

Firstly, a good many sermons would be improved with pruning, even if it were not the case that conditions require it. Three and a half centuries ago, Pascal wrote a letter to a friend which ended: 'I have made this longer than usual, only because I have not had time to make it shorter.'[15] There is a lesson there for all of us. Perhaps today's impatience with long sermons will be the platform for more effective preaching tomorrow. Saying less, but saying it more lucidly and memorably than before, is a strategy many preachers would be wise to adopt.

It is encouraging to discover that, even in the days when long sermons were the norm, the greatest preachers found sermon length a problem. Asked how long he normally took to deliver a sermon, the mighty Sangster was reluctant to say. His wife answered for him: on a Sunday evening at Westminster Central Hall, a sermon would last about forty-five minutes. The questioner, who happened to be the Governor General of Ireland, was stunned. 'Does anybody come?' he asked.[16] The answer was, of course, that thousands did. Whether they would do so today is open to question. Yes, there are still preachers who can hold a church congregation spellbound at great length, but they are few. Most of us must settle for brevity and devote ourselves to the carefully constructed, finely-tuned, short sermon.

Such a sermon requires no less preparation than a long one. The same ingredients go into the mixture: extensive reading, careful reflection and prayer. If any one of those is neglected, the cake will not rise. It is harder to find enough time for all three than once it was because the conditions in which sermons are cooked up have changed.

There was a time when it was easier than now for preachers to shut themselves away to study, think and pray. The pressures of the modern lifestyle do not lend themselves to quiet contemplation. All sorts of social changes have made it so, not the least of which has been the sharing of responsibilities in the home. Where both partners in a relationship go out to work, and each accepts an equal share of responsibility in caring for the home and raising children, it is hard for someone to spend hours on sermon preparation. A deep sense of guilt may overcome a person who pores over some biblical passage while domestic chaos rings in his or her ears. The half-baked, ill-thought-out, hastily constructed sermon is not necessarily the outcome of a preacher's lack of motivation. 'It's finding the time that's a struggle,' said one preacher on trial, 'sometimes the family just doesn't understand.' As with all forms of Christian commitment, whoever would preach must count the cost, and involve others who are affected in that process.

Secondly, the way ahead requires us to accept that the days when Methodist folk came to church simply to hear a good sermon and sing the hymns of Wesley and Watts are over. There is, of course, a sizeable remnant in every congregation which yearns for things as they used to be, but many people, and especially parents anxious that their children remain within the life of the church, seek a more varied diet. That is not to diminish the importance of the sermon, whose impact may well be enhanced by being placed in a variegated context. Those who see diversification in worship as a threat to the status of the sermon misunderstand what the Lord is about. Multimedia worship facilities are *aids* to preaching, not *substitutes* for it. Some churches have yet to grasp the point, and we preachers must stand our ground in the new millennium for the preservation of the sermon at the heart of worship.

Many preachers are able and willing to experiment with diversification, whereby a variety of activities beyond traditional ones provide a framework for preaching. But the abilities required are different from those needed in the days of the hymn sandwich. Today's preachers are no longer as reliant as were their predecessors upon their own oratorical and associated skills: they are managers of the skills of others. Dance, drama and praise bands are becoming regular features of Christian worship, as is the use of sophisticated equipment to produce stunning visual and aural effects. Today's preacher must combine an understanding of electronics with the skills of a theatre manager and the stamina of a roadie. He or she must also possess the negotiating prowess of a shop steward in dealing with the different interest groups contributing to diversified worship. Transforming a good idea, involving a variety of ways of representing and exploring the gospel, into a coherent act of worship, is enormously demanding. Done badly, it has led worshippers to ask, 'What was that pantomime all about?' Done well, it powerfully supports the preacher's pulpit performance.

Thirdly, we preachers must recognise that our lustre has faded. Martyn Lloyd-Jones and his contemporaries were the last generation of those whose pulpit authority went largely unquestioned among those who flocked to hear them, although even for them the tide of ready acceptance of their opinions as matters of theological fact was on the turn. A young man with a keen but questioning interest in the Christian faith went on a course of Bible study. He had for some time been struggling with the Nativity narratives, and some of the more chauvinistic teachings of St Paul. At the end of the course, he decided to ask for a note to preach. He said: 'I'm much happier now that I know what you *don't* have to believe. What a relief.' And so say a good many young people in the church today, and some not so young. That is not to say, of course, that there are no longer any mighty truths for the preacher to proclaim. My own journey in teaching and preaching the gospel has involved a retreat from the marshland of a hundred certainties to the firm ground of a few unshakeable beliefs. Finding firm ground, and helping others to do the same, is one of the most exciting aspects of pulpit performance.

A powerful alternative to preaching in the context of a church service is the annual gathering at a residential venue of thousands of the Christian faithful, and their friends and relations, for a spiritual wind-up. The Spring Harvest and Easter People events, and others like them, bring together numbers like those that once filled the great preaching places where the old pulpit masters operated. Of the many activities that take place on such occasions, those who attend invariably speak enthusiastically about the power of the preaching. But, while the contribution of such events to the preservation and promotion of the preacher's role can be significant, the wind-up can lead to a mighty let-down if those who attend return to uninspired churches where change is about as welcome as death-watch beetle in the timbers.

Notwithstanding the context within which preaching takes place, its purpose remains constant. When Calvin wrote that, when the gospel is preached, it is as if God himself is summoning us, he expressed a timeless truth that is not dependent on the many and changing situations in which preaching occurs. Whatever happens to patterns of worship, the preacher remains responsible for giving voice to God's summons, and for bringing about a response among those who have ears to hear.

3

THE PREACHER
AS PROPHET

Addressing members of the Royal Society of Arts in a lecture on the subject of communication in modern society, Sir David Puttnam told the story of a little girl who had a geography test in school. Pupils were given a list of countries and asked to tick those in which an elephant would be found. The little girl wrote: 'This is a silly question. Elephants are much too big and much too clever to get lost in the first place'.[1]

Sir David, who has since become Lord Puttnam, used this story to make a point about the information society in which we now live. We are, he argued, required to look at questions in a new way, with a completely different set of attitudes, rather as children do with those asked by adults. In particular, in looking into the future, we should be asking ourselves not what the world will be like next year or the year after, but in twenty, fifty or even a hundred years.

In his or her prophetic role, the preacher has always been called upon to take a longer view than contemporaries. The Old Testament prophets often suffered for having a better idea of which way the wind was blowing than those around them. Discerning future disasters as evidence of God's judgement on a faithless nation, their place in public opinion polls was not infrequently 'the pits'. Jeremiah was thrown into one.

The average preacher would probably regard the title 'prophet' as a somewhat grandiose description of his or her role. While a few of those who are most highly acclaimed have been seen as exercising prophetic ministries, the rest would not expect to be regarded in that light. They play in a lower league than the preachers' premiership. While Donald Soper was quite often described as a prophet during his mighty ministry in the open air at Tower Hill and Hyde Park, most others would not expect to be so named.

But if one looks back to Moses, the founder of the prophetic tradition, one sees that some, if not all, his qualifications are found in many preachers. He received a personal call from God; he possessed an awareness and understanding of history; he had a concern for the moral and social welfare of his contemporaries; most important of all, he combined proclamation and prediction in his message. If, as biblical scholars assert, those are the marks of a prophet, they may be possessed at all levels of preaching, from the Soperian heights to the lowlands where lesser pulpit persons operate.

Proclaiming the gospel, and predicting the outcome of its being believed or rejected, is a feature of many sermons. A preacher who fails to offer the gospel, and relate it to the present and future condition of individuals and the world, neglects to do what a sermon is supposed to do.

But the prophetic style which derives from the Old Testament commitment to pronouncing God's judgement on the unfaithful is becoming rare, and the reason is not hard to discern. We live at a time when it is no longer generally acceptable for one person to pass judgement on the beliefs, appetites or lifestyle of another. In our pluralist, inclusive, multicultural, multifaith and no-faith-in-anything-very-much society, the philosophy most widely propounded is that everyone's opinion and way of life is as good as everyone else's.

Those who oppose the passing of judgement by one person on another often turn to John Stuart Mill's brilliant essay 'On Liberty', first published in 1859, to justify their position. As a young undergraduate at the London School of Economics and Political Science several decades ago, the present writer grasped to himself with bands of steel Mill's famous assertion: 'The sole end for which mankind are warranted, individually or collectively, in interfering with the liberty of action of any of their number, is self-protection.'[2] In my salad days, my interpretation of that led me to welcome it as a release from most constraints. Interfering with anyone's freedom to do just what they liked was not to be tolerated. It was easy to overlook Mill's insistence that interference was entirely warranted as a means to protect the individual from the tyranny of the majority. His immortal words on the subject have stood, and will forever stand, the test of time:

> If all mankind minus one, were of one opinion, and only one person were of the contrary opinion, mankind would be no more justified in silencing that one person, than he, if he had the power, would be justified in silencing mankind.[3]

Mill's words speak directly to the condition of the West in this day and age. The prophetic voice of judgement has been largely silenced by the most powerful means of communication ever devised. Television sends directly into people's homes messages which are largely hostile to traditional Christian values. Blasphemous language, sexual promiscuity and drunkenness are daily depicted as normal. At Christmas 1998, the programme which had the largest number of viewers was *Men Behaving Badly*, a show portraying unsavoury human conduct as merely a matter of amusement. Although the BBC was forced to admit that the edition in question was perhaps not suitable for Christmas family viewing, any suggestion that the weekly diet of dissolute goings-on it provides might promote immoral behaviour would doubtless be laughed to scorn by its regular audience. In the spring of 1999, *The Times* welcomed a re-run of the series by describing it as all good, filthy fun (*sic*).[4] It was, asserted that once distinguished newspaper, one of the *most popular* sitcoms of the Nineties. That, it seemed, was the end of any argument about it. The tyranny of the majority is almost absolute in a world where television viewing is the dominant leisure activity.

The preacher as prophet stands over against the adoption of hedonism in contemporary society. He or she calls hearers to repentance and a new way of life because only by that means can disaster be avoided. The message is as old as the hills, yet new to each generation of sinners. But the voice of the prophetic preacher who is ready and willing to charge our society with sin, and demand repentance before God's retribution arrives, is not much heard. It rings out most clearly from black churches, from preachers like the Most Reverend Prophetess Fidelia Onkyuku-Opukiri. She studied theology at the University of Birmingham and is an executive member of the Centre for Black and White Christian Partnership, a title which is in itself prophetic, is it not? Her preaching is anchored in scripture and exegetical in its development. Despite her commitment to social justice and racial equality, she does not wander into the territory of political polemic. Her prophetic vision arises from the Bible, not a political agenda.

So, what prophecies does this modern prophetess offer? In a sermon on the opening verses of John 15, she explains the allegory of Jesus as the true vine.[5] Dealing with the fruits that grow from our being the branches of the vine, she says that the Holy Spirit has revealed to her that they are three. The first is the ability to earn our living in the conviction that everything we receive comes from God; the second is, by the grace of God and the power of Christ's redeeming blood, to live righteous lives; the third is to be able to overcome satanic forces. The gospel of personal salvation is the foundation on which this kind of preaching is based. It is prophetic in that it makes an assessment of our present condition and points the way forward to a life lived with confidence in God's promises in scripture.

While less dramatic than that of the prophetess Fidelia, most preaching has prophetic elements. A good test of any sermon is to ask three questions of it:

1. Does it address people's needs where they are, and those of the world in which they live?

2. Does it make known God's grace, by which individuals and thereby the world community may be changed?

3. Does it reveal and glorify a future determined by the power and purposes of God?

These elements of prophetic preaching are found severally in the words of all the great prophets of the Old Testament, in the preaching of the gospel as it is recorded in Acts, and in the letters of Paul and others. Human needs are addressed, God's grace made known and the nature of his future kingdom revealed.

It is important to recognise that prophetic ministry is not about forecasting the future. It will involve prediction, but revealing what the days or years ahead may hold is not its purpose: it is merely a means of driving home what needs to be done in the present. Telling a child that, if it plays with fire, it will burn, is prophetic guidance aimed at avoiding self-immolation. Similarly, the preacher's prophecy of disaster is made to help people avoid it. Prediction of good things ahead is, similarly, not a statement of inevitability but an encouragement to strive to live God's way. In short, prophecy aims at making hearers aware of what will follow from the dreams they dream, the hopes they hold, the ambitions they accumulate and the allegiances they enter into. What biblical scholars call prophetic awareness, be it related to the grand sweep of world history, or the agony and ecstasy of daily life for the individual, is a feature of all great preaching.

In one of the many letters on which his literary reputation rests, Horace Walpole wrote in 1775: 'The wisest prophets make sure of the event first.'[6] Perhaps he got the idea from his father. Robert Walpole, England's first Prime Minister, is regarded by historians as a man of acute political judgement, the wisdom of whose advice in 1743 not to get involved in the War of the Austrian Succession was ignored at great cost. He it was who foresaw the outcome of a foolhardy strategy. It is perhaps not without point that his prediction, though proved accurate in the event, cost him his office at the time because the popular mood was against him. So it may be with the political prophet, as with the theological one.

Did Horace Walpole misread the basis of his father's perceptivity and believe that he had access to some visionary awareness denied to others? There were certainly those involved in the cut and thrust of eighteenth century politics who saw Robert Walpole as extraordinarily able in his prediction of outcomes. But the notion of prophecy as supernatural foreknowledge is almost certainly not what Horace Walpole had in mind. In the cynical context of eighteenth century Europe, he was merely proposing a strategy for political success.

Making sure you know what the future holds is not part of the prophetic ministry of the preacher. Only God knows, and what the preacher does is try, with a greater degree of humility than certainty, to discern what God intends.

But that is not to say that prophetic awareness is a speculative exercise bereft of certainty. One of the greatest of the ancient prophets has shown the preacher the way in this regard. Isaiah, in relaying God's words to the Hebrews during their captivity in Babylon, had this message:

> I am God, and there is no one like me, declaring the end from the beginning and from ancient times things not yet done, saying, 'My purpose shall stand and I will fulfil my intention.'
>
> Isaiah 46:9-10

The certainty of God's eventual victory is the immovable foundation of the preacher's prophetic message. Over against it, he or she sets the madness of reliance on human wisdom to solve the world's problems, and the everyday struggles of the individual. 'Has not God made foolish the wisdom of the world?' wrote Paul (1 Corinthians 1:20). It is a rhetorical question. Humanity's attempts to determine the way ahead have not resolved the human condition; but we are not yet ready to give up running our own show.

In his fine novel, *Captain Corelli's Mandolin*, set in the Greek island of Cephallonia during the 1939-45 war, Louis de Bernières has one character assert: 'The British plan everything in retrospect, so it always looks as though everything occurred as they intended.' Some preachers are certainly adept at what might be called retrospective prophetic awareness. Only after an event has occurred do they discern God's hand at work. But perhaps perceiving divine activity after the event – and sometimes long after – is one of God's gifts to us as we advance in faith.

One of the true wonders of preaching is the extent to which what is heard from the pulpit is different from what has been said, and more powerful in its impact. Many preachers have been surprised to be thanked for the support and guidance given by a message they were not aware of having delivered. 'That word about showing your family you love them every day was for me,' said the father who put his wife and three young children well below his interest in his batting average, 'I'm going to spend more time with them.' Disconcerted, I resisted telling him I had said nothing about family life. If he had received a message he needed to hear, who was the preacher to criticise him for nodding off or failing to follow the sermon properly? Only after having a similar experience many times did I realise that, far from worshippers nodding off or losing track, they were having the ears of their hearts opened by the Lord.

Every good cook knows that a really tasty home-made cake has had a secret ingredient stirred into it, namely love for those who will eat it. In his poem 'The Apple Dumpling', D H Lawrence relates this to the teaching of Jesus in Luke 6:38. He says that, if someone baking a dumpling kneads the dough with affection, and thinks with kindly compassion about those who will sit and eat it, then good is the dumpling, happy those who share it and content the person who made it. So, he concludes, 'Give and it will be given to you is still the truth about life.' Every powerful sermon has a secret ingredient. If the preacher's loving concern for those who will hear it is great enough, the Lord will knead into it a message for each and every one. When that awesome discovery first dawns on a preacher, it makes a mighty difference to his or her sermon preparation.

The famous ballet dancer, Rudolf Nureyev, was asked by a media critic at the end of the performance of a new ballet to explain its meaning in a sentence. 'If I could explain it in a sentence,' he replied, 'there would be no need for the dance.' God's message in a sermon is not to be explained in a sentence, nor even in all the sentences of which it is constituted. As the message of the dance amounts to more than the steps of the dancer, be they ever so many, and brilliantly executed, so what is communicated through that dramatic activity we call preaching amounts to a great deal more than the words spoken. He who is Lord of the dance is also Lord of the pulpit.

When Jesus taught in the synagogue at Nazareth, some objected because, in their eyes, he was a nobody. By way of a response, Jesus offered a message every preacher knows well (Matthew 13:57): 'Prophets are not without honour except in their own country.' The people of India have a similar saying: 'There is always a shadow near the lamp.' Only at a distance can the light be fully appreciated. But undue weight should not be placed on this teaching. One of the advantages an ordained minister usually has over a lay preacher is closer knowledge of his or her congregations. In the Methodist Church, most ministers preach regularly to people whose personal problems are familiar to them. By comparison, the local preacher is on a theological hike that may involve visiting a congregation no more than once a quarter. 'We thought you'd left the district,' said an ancient worshipper to a local preacher whom she thought was not up to much. It was the note of disappointment in her voice the young man found distressing. In due course, he emerged from the chrysalis of faltering pulpit performance to become a preacher with a powerful prophetic awareness. The preacher as prophet is almost always someone of considerable maturity. Prophetic strength comes with that process which Paul describes as sanctification.

Thomas Kingsmill Abbott's 1885 translation of Kant's *Introduction to Logic* begins:

> Everything in nature, whether in the animate or inanimate world, takes place according to rules, although we do not always know these rules. Water falls according to the laws of gravity and in animals locomotion also takes place according to rules. The fish in the water, the bird in the air, moves according to rules. All nature, indeed, is nothing but a combination of phenomena which follow rules; and nowhere is there any irregularity. When we think we find any such, we can only say that the rules are unknown.[7]

Kant makes no reference to religion in his treatise, but what he says is not inconsistent with the Christian gospel. We believe that God's creation is rational and subject to laws that govern the way it works. As time has advanced, more and more laws have been discovered and, if the writings of such as Stephen Hawking are to be believed, we are not far from establishing what scientists call a whole theory of the universe – an explanation of the cosmos that provides a coherent statement of origins, and of how all parts of creation relate to all other parts.

People have forever struggled to make sense of the universe in which this small planet finds its place, and of the life forms that walk and run, creep and crawl, grow and die upon and below its surface, and in its mighty seas. The more that has been discovered, the greater the sense of awe the advances of science have generated. Primitive belief in a flat earth and a creative overlord located in the blue skies above was easier to grasp than anything we are now called to comprehend, but it diminished God.

We now know, or think we know, that the Sun is 100 million miles from planet Earth. If that figure seems beyond our comprehension, it is only the beginning of the numbers game. Of the nine planets which orbit the Sun in the solar system, the furthest away, Pluto, is forty times as distant from it as Earth. Beyond that, scientists have had to invent the concept of light years to explain themselves. Light travels at about 186,000 miles a second. A light year is the distance light travels at that speed in one year. The galaxy of 100 billion stars in a spiral disc we call the Milky Way, which we can see in the sky above us on a clear night, is 100,000 light years in diameter. There are many other galaxies of stars in the universe stretching billions of light years into space.

The human mind finds it impossible to grasp the extent of what is out there. The moon landing, acclaimed as a giant leap for mankind, was nothing of the kind. It was more like a child's first experience of the sea when it places a tiny foot in one of the world's vast oceans. Unless time travel proves a possibility, we will never be able to explore our own solar system, let alone anything beyond. It all adds to the impact of the psalmist's words:

> How weighty to me are your thoughts, O God! How vast is the sum of them! I try to count them – they are more than the sand; I come to the end – I am still with you.
>
> (Psalm 139:17-18).

We now know there are more stars in the universe than all the grains of sand on planet Earth. In contemplating the extent of the mind of God, the psalmist was limited to what he knew. His best attempt at finding a comparator was the number of grains of sand in the deserts he trod and on the shores of the seas he knew. But modern astronomy has taken us beyond that. It tells us that there is nothing on our planet that can be compared with the dimensions of the Creator's mind.

There was a time when the Christian church felt threatened by the advance of scientific knowledge, but it ought not to be so in this day and age because, as our understanding of origins has increased, and of how things have come to be as they are, our perception of the originator has surely grown as well. William Blake asked of the tiger, 'Did he who made the lamb make thee?' With the onward march of human understanding of the cosmos has come an increasingly awesome appreciation of the question 'Did he who made all that make me?'

In his book, *God, the Big Bang and Stephen Hawking,* David Wilkinson, a Methodist minister with a doctorate in astrophysics, relates the story of President Roosevelt of the United States who followed a nightly ritual to prevent his becoming too proud. Before going to bed, he would go outside and look into the sky. He would say to himself, 'One of those lights is the spiral galaxy of Andromeda. It contains one hundred billion stars, each the size of our own Sun. It is one of one hundred billion galaxies in the universe, each as large as our own Milky Way.' He would then pause and make an evaluation: 'Now I feel small enough, I can go to bed'.[8]

In the prophetic role, the preacher surely has something to say about all this. Theology being the study of God and his relationship with his creation, the arrival of a whole theory of the universe presents an opportunity and a responsibility to press home prophetic awareness of the grace of God. As we uncover more and more of what Kant called the rules which explain the natural world, so the incomprehensible extent of God's grace towards us grows. Not even the invention of light years is sufficient to measure it.

4

THE SEARCHER, THE SCHOLAR AND THE AXE-GRINDER

There are many different kinds of preacher. They reflect the diversity of individuals across the face of the earth. Carl Sandberg pictures a man going out into the world to make his fortune and returning, after many adventures, bearing the same unique thumb print, different from all others, as the day he kissed his mother goodbye. 'Somewhere,' writes Sandberg, 'there is a Great God of Thumbs who can tell the inside story of this.'[1]

Preachers being part of the story, each will have his or her own approach and style in the pulpit. When Edmund Burke observed that most pious discourses were calculated for the benefit of the preacher rather than the edification of those listening, he was being typically cynical. But all sermons arise in part from the background, interests and concerns of the preacher rather than those of the congregation. The influences which shape those who proclaim the gospel are many and varied. What was their childhood experience of religion? How did they come to hear God's call to preach? Which preacher is their model? What is their attitude towards, and understanding of, church doctrine? What style and content of training prepared them for the pulpit? What theological position do they take up with respect to the authority of the Bible? Is the preacher a man or a woman? Have they come to the pulpit in their salad days, in the prime of life or with silver in their hair and the first signs of their little grey cells packing up? Which football team do they support?

Stan Baker was a genuine London east-ender. His attitude to life on Sundays was hugely affected by what had happened the previous afternoon at Upton Park, the home of West Ham United Football Club. That was the case even after he moved out of London with his family to live in Kent. As a Methodist local preacher, he was greatly loved in the chapels in and around Tonbridge, not least because he led prayer in such a powerful way that he was able to reach right into people's hearts. But sometimes Stan needed a bit of cheering up in the vestry before a service if the Hammers had been hammered on Saturday. Walking with me to chapel one evening, he asked what the world was coming to. I thought he was worrying about the starving millions of Africa but no, he was heartbroken because the Hammers had been beaten 3-0 at home by Arsenal. It was a humiliation Stan found hard to bear. Fortunately, he wasn't preaching that evening or the congregation would have been in for a gloomy time of it.

When we know what influences have shaped a preacher, we will know something of where he or she is coming from. But we are unlikely ever to know enough fully to understand what experiences have formulated the faith of any man or woman. Each of us is destined to remain something of a mystery to those around us. Arthur Koestler touches on this in his contribution to *The God That Failed*, a collection of essays by prominent writers who joined the Communist Party in the 1930s and subsequently resigned from it when they became disillusioned. What Koestler has to say in his essay is relevant to the matter of how a man or woman arrives at the point of wanting to preach the gospel:

> A faith is not acquired by reasoning. One does not fall in love with a woman, or enter the womb of a church, as a result of logical persuasion. Reason may defend an act of faith, but only after the act has been

committed, and the man committed to the act. Persuasion may play a part in a man's conversion; but only the part of bringing to its full conscious climax a process which has been maturing in regions where no persuasion can penetrate. A faith is not acquired; it grows like a tree. Its crown points to the sky; its roots grow downward into the past and are nourished by the dark sap of the ancestral humus.[2]

A diversity of experiences, some conscious and highly memorable, others buried deep in the dark sap of scarce remembered events, bring a man or woman to the point of feeling compelled to proclaim the gospel. The words preachers use, the feelings they have and the outcomes they expect as they lead worship will therefore vary greatly. What follows is an analysis of three types of preacher. They are chosen because there is something of each of them in all preachers.

The Searcher

The searcher-preacher uses preaching as a route by which to pursue his or her search for faith. That is not a sign of weakness. John Wesley believed that proclaiming the gospel would lead to a strengthening of a preacher's belief, and many have found it to be so.

Any experienced teacher will tell you that there's nothing like teaching your subject to develop your understanding of it. Mind you, young people have been taught some cock-eyed things while a newcomer has been getting to grips with the art and science of teaching. In my days as an examiner of teachers in training, I observed a lesson in economics in which the teacher was dealing with the different documents used in commercial transactions. He carefully explained that, when a ship's cargo has been placed aboard, a document called 'a bill of loading' is issued. He wrote it on the board and told the class to make sure and get it into their heads. When I pointed out to him afterwards that the correct name of the document was 'a bill of lading', from the Middle English verb to lade, meaning to place a burden on a vehicle or person or beast of burden, hence the term laden, he looked astonished and said: 'That's interesting. I never knew that. I always thought the text-book had got the spelling wrong.' Whatever that young economics teacher forgets in the future, he is destined to be an authority on the spelling, the meaning and the derivation of the term 'bill of lading'.

Young searcher-preachers sometimes have an inclination to offer cock-eyed ideas from the pulpit. A confident grasp of theology being as yet beyond their ken, they are inclined to try out whatever ideas occur to them. Their sermons take on some of the features of learning to ride a two-wheeler bike. The scriptural exegesis is a bit wobbly, the sense of direction erratic and the likelihood that they are about to fall off causes a mood of uneasiness in the congregation.

It is of no great help to the preacher to be six feet or more above contradiction when preaching, and to have little or no challenge when subsequently outside the safety of the pulpit. There is a case to be made for all preachers to make themselves available for question and answer sessions arising from their preaching of the gospel, or failure to preach it. It is not just newcomers to the pulpit who need to be assessed; some of the old guard long ago ceased to deliver the gospel goods worthily. Shame to the preacher who announced to his congregation: 'It's Advent Sunday so this is the sermon I've fished out of my files.' He who said that hadn't even bothered to update his material, which contained references to events in the news so out of date that we all knew he hadn't even studied his old sermon notes before coming to church. Had he done so, he would surely have realised he was about to make a fool of himself. He had stopped searching; finished with studying the gospel to make new discoveries about it; turned preaching into a purely mechanistic activity like the washing or the ironing, which can be done with your mind on something else.

Sadly, there are a good many experienced preachers whose pulpit offerings show no evidence of their still being on a journey of discovery. They appear not to have had a new thought about the gospel, or a new way of expressing it, for a very long time. They have a deadening effect on congregations, not an enlivening one. Ralph Waldo Emerson wrote the following in his journal in 1832 about his own efforts:

> The sermon which I write inquisitive of truth is good a year after, but that which is written because a sermon must be writ is musty the next day.

It is alleged that Adam was somewhat philosophical as he left the Garden of Eden. 'My dear,' said he to Eve, 'we live in an age of transition.' The searcher-preacher recognises that he or she is forever in transition. The need to continue to explore theological issues in the light of new research, and of world events, is a fundamental obligation. John Milton wrote in his *Doctrine and Discipline* that theology is an exercise in exploration from which those expounding the gospel must never rest. He said this: 'To be still searching what we know not by what we know, still closing up truth to truth as we find it, this is the golden rule in theology as in arithmetic.'[3]

In 1977, the year of the Queen's silver jubilee, *The Times Educational Supplement* published a cartoon which caused great amusement in school staff rooms, and some unease as well. It showed one teacher saying to another: 'I thought I would get out my old teaching notes from twenty-five years ago and have a look at what I was teaching then, but I discovered I was still using them.' There is, of course, nothing wrong with a preacher using the same sermon theme for a quarter of a century, but the presentation should surely show some growth and development in his or her thinking; some discovery of new illustrations in the course of study and experience; some evidence of progress in pursuit of truth.

In his book, *The Ascent of Man*, Jacob Bronowski makes two observations which seem to me to have relevance to the position of the preacher as a searcher after truth. First, Bronowski asserts that human achievement is not a museum of finished constructions but a progress. He warns against any generation admiring its own discoveries as if they might be the last word. There was a time, he reminds us, when the medieval clocks of Europe were thought to say all that it would ever be necessary to say about the heavens. Now we smile at such naivety. But the day will surely come when our descendants will smile at us. Secondly, Bronowski emphasises that man is unique among animals because he is not only a figure in the landscape but a shaper of it. He goes on:

> Among the multitude of animals that scamper, fly, burrow and swim around us, man is the only one that is not locked into his environment. His imagination, his reason, his emotional subtlety and toughness, make it possible for him not to accept the environment but to change it.[4]

What might be called the ascent of the searcher-preacher is a process which takes place within the framework which Bronowski draws. He or she recognises that the last theological word has not been spoken; that the reality of God is not yet by any means completely clear to us; that our relationship with him – and her? – is a slow revelation, not an accomplished fact. In short, theology is no more a museum of finished constructions than is human achievement. Furthermore, we have the power to shape our theological environment; our understanding of God; our commitment to his purposes.

It is one of the paradoxes of God's salvation plan, made known in scripture and carried into effect in the person of Jesus, that it reveals God's nature but leaves us with a multitude of unanswered questions. As the ascent of man the scientist progresses, the extent and complexity of God's creation becomes more amazing to us. It makes us increasingly aware of how slight is our grasp of what

God is really like. If one were to take a drawing pin and press it into the side of an elephant, the size of the dent in relation to the whole elephant would be a measure of the extent of our knowledge of God in relation to all there is to be known about him. But that is just as well. As the great medieval scholar Peter Abelard once observed, if we understood, we would think ourselves to be God.

The history of the church is the story of humankind's yearning to understand. But confrontation between holders of differing opinions has sometimes become almost as much a struggle for power as a search for truth. The New Testament displays the inclination of the early church to enter into disputation at the drop of a doctrinal hat, sometimes as part of a power struggle.

The conflict between Peter and Paul on the issue of circumcision was a battle for supremacy between two strong-willed men as well as a disagreement over doctrine. 'When Peter came to Antioch, I opposed him to his face, because he was clearly in the wrong,' wrote Paul in his letter to the Galatians (2:11, NIV). Had television been available, the two antagonists would no doubt have appeared on the six o'clock news on Antioch Rediffusion. Fortunately for us, Paul was successful in establishing that Christians were not bound by Jewish religious customs. But for his forcefulness, the early church might have been torn apart. Without doubt, there are times when the church must put its doctrinal foot down.

The foot came down less firmly when the church struggled to agree a doctrine of the person of Christ – an unambiguous statement reconciling his humanity and his divinity. In the debates which occupied theologians in the first four centuries of the church's life, Athanasius emerged as the man most able to say what needed to be said and his view was adopted at the Council of Nicea in 325, which adopted the Nicene Creed we use today. Even so, arguments continued and the Council of Chalcedon in 451 set about explaining exactly what the holy fathers of Nicea had meant, attempting to eliminate all further doubts. The outcome was the following declaration:

We, then, following the holy Fathers, all with one consent, teach men to confess one and the same Son, our Lord Jesus Christ, the same perfect in Godhead and also perfect in manhood; truly God and truly man, of a reasonable soul and body; consubstantial with the Father according to the Godhead, and consubstantial with us according to the manhood; in all things like unto us without sin; begotten before all ages of the Father according to the Godhead, and in these latter days, for us and for our salvation, born of the Virgin Mary, the Mother of God, according to the manhood; one and the same Christ, Son, Lord, Only-begotten, in two natures, inconfusedly, unchangeably, indivisibly, inseparably, the distinction of natures being by no means taken away by the union, but rather the property of each nature being preserved and concurring in one person, and one substance, not parted or divided into two persons, but one and the same Son and only-begotten, God the Word, the Lord Jesus Christ; as the prophets from the beginning have declared concerning Him, and as the Lord Jesus Christ Himself has taught us, and the creed of the holy Fathers has been handed down to us.

In his *Groundwork of Theology*, John Stacey says of this statement: 'This then was, and is, the orthodox Christian position.'[5] But surely a good deal of explaining would need to be done before today's congregations would be able to make head or tail of it.

Doctrinal disputes and struggles for power have continued to beset the church down the centuries. The great schism between the churches of the East and those of the West in 1054 introduced separationism as a new outcome – the tendency of the church to fragment and sub-divide. The process continued in the Reformation and accelerated with the eruption of nonconformity in its many manifestations. The multiplicity of denominational groups at the beginning of the third millennium, and of groups which reject denominational labels, constitutes the eighth wonder of the world and suggests that Christians enjoy nothing so much as disagreeing with one another.

In a speech made in America in the spring of 1999, the Archbishop of Canterbury, George Carey, warned Anglicans of serious difficulties arising from what he saw as increasingly diverse doctrines being espoused by members.[6] He asserted that the traditions which had held Anglicans together since the Reformation were being increasingly ignored. 'Common prayer, common ministry, common history,' he said, 'have become less and less influential in our individual churches.' Clearly aware of searchers in his audience, he said that he recognised what he called 'the validity of everyone's search', but insisted that not all views or propositions were acceptable. Doubtless his hearers in Charleston, a city which suffered a good deal in the American Civil War, would have agreed with him. However, with equal lack of doubt, there would have been a considerable divergence of views as to which propositions were to be considered acceptable, and which not. Thus, the civil war between conservatives and liberals across the denominations both sides of the Atlantic grows apace.

Just as the growth of scientific awareness has made us increasingly aware of how much we have yet to discover about the nature and extent of God's creation, so the efforts of the church over the past thousand years to establish clear, comprehensive doctrines, creeds and articles of faith have helped us to realise that, in doing so, we attempt to interpret the incomprehensible; to constrain within the limits of human language revelations which are beyond human understanding; to confine the divine. But yesterday's definition of what a Christian knows and believes, and the social consequences flowing from that knowledge and belief, is soon overtaken by new scholarship, changing social conditions and – God forgive us – fresh developments in the crash and sway of the ecclesiastical power struggle. The fact that Anglican ordinands for years assented to the Thirty-nine Articles with their tongues in their cheeks illustrates the temporary nature of a good deal that passes for religious certainty. Nowadays, those newly priested still have publicly to sign a document indicating their assent to the historic formularies of the Church of England at the conclusion of their first licensing service, but what those formularies are is no longer spelled out. 'It means,' said an Anglican friend preparing for ordination, 'you can decide for yourself, inside your own head, what you are agreeing to.'

Against that background, what service to worshippers does the searcher-preacher perform? 'He's no help to me,' said an Anglican friend of a particular priest, 'he asks questions but doesn't give us the answers. He muddles me up.' Those who speak in that way prefer to have everything laid down for them. They tend to gravitate to Christian fellowships where what used to be called fundamentalist preaching takes place. Interestingly, in an age when old social and moral codes are breaking down, churches where didactic preaching is practised are growing, while others decline. People want to be told the old, old theological story. They feel threatened by suggestions that they should think new thoughts, explore new interpretations of scripture and acknowledge that theology is not a museum of finished constructions. What the searcher-preacher does is give comfort and encouragement to those who have anxieties about the gospel. He or she makes doubt an authentic, acceptable, permanent feature of the Christian's pilgrimage.

Searcher-preachers encourage congregations to search out for themselves the answers to their questions. They make great demands on them, requiring them to think for themselves; study the Bible for themselves; pray constantly; come to different conclusions among themselves, and live with that. Searcher-preachers send their congregations out into their daily lives searching, always searching for more of the truth.

John Dryden, who was born in 1631 and died in 1700, lived through a time of huge doctrinal struggles under

Stuart kings, and in Oliver Cromwell's military state. Experiencing the clash and sway of conflicting religious beliefs, Dryden wrote:

> But since men will believe more than they need,
> And every man will make himself a creed,
> In doubtful questions, 'tis the safest way,
> To learn what unsuspected ancients say.[7]

There's little doubt that we each have our own creed, rarely if ever expressed, and very likely containing some strange and unnecessary beliefs. But Dryden's remedy, to turn to the credal utterances of the ancients, seems not to meet the needs of a good many Christians today. We each have to find whatever truth there is to be discovered for ourselves.

So is there no room for certainty in the pulpit? The certainty the preacher offers is that, come what may, be our doubts ever so great, be the things we are sure about ever so few, and becoming fewer as we unload surplus theological baggage under the searcher-preacher's influence, the God we worship is a creator whose nature is endless, enduring, indestructible love. The uncertainties the searcher-preacher explores have to do with the implications of that for the church, for the world and for the individual. Anyone who stands in the pulpit proclaiming that all the answers in that territory are blindingly obvious is not caring for the Lord's sheep but leading them up the garden path.

The Scholar

Some preachers use the pulpit as a lecture platform, from which they deliver learned discourses on theological issues. Preparing to hear one such on a visit to a church in an unfamiliar part of the Methodist connexion, the present writer was nudged by the person sitting next to him and warned: 'Just you watch when he comes in. He'll have a pile of books up to his chin.' It was, of course, an exaggeration. The pile fell at least two books short of the preacher's jawline.

The scholar has an honourable place in the heritage of preaching. John Calvin, from whom all modern preachers are descended, simply carried his technique as a university teacher into the pulpit. Indeed, where would the church be without its scholar-preachers? It is they upon whom we depend to advance our theological understanding in an age when belief in God is widely neglected and often dismissed.

But those who carry scholarliness into the pulpit must guard against lifting off into the theological stratosphere, leaving everybody else gazing in uncomprehending wonderment at the smoke trail left behind. Learned occupants of the pulpit must also resist the temptation to flaunt their cleverness at the expense of their hearers' faith. David Jenkins, when Bishop of Durham, was accused of that. His skilful demolition job on the significance some Christians attach to the bodily Resurrection caused an uproar. His assertion that Christian faith ought not to depend on a conjuring trick with bones doubtless went down well in discussion at high table among Oxbridge dons, but was hardly helpful to Mrs Buggins, a faithful servant of the Lord for sixty years at her local parish church, who shook her head in incredulity when she read about it in the newspapers. The media were content to ignore, or maybe unable to understand, the important point David Jenkins was making, namely that concentrating on what happened to the body of Jesus was to miss the true glory of the Easter message. Rattling on about a skeleton in the bishop's cupboard made far better copy.

Intellectual analysis of Christian doctrine has an important part to play in the development of Christian faith. David Jenkins was right to insist that it cannot be sustained simply on the basis of unthinking literal acceptance of scripture. It was his brilliantly clever way of saying it that caused distress because it took insufficient account of the needs of the many different sorts and conditions of people who would hear it. His cleverness confounded his purpose by damaging the roots of some people's faith. Here lies a lesson for the scholar-preacher to learn: scholarship must be the servant, not the master, of the gospel message. It must be used with tender loving care for the unscholarly. Scripture tells us that one of the characteristics of love is that it is never puffed up. That is a message of which all preachers should take heed, and not least the most learned and scholarly in their ranks.

Notwithstanding the tendency of some scholar-preachers to concentrate more heavily on scholarship than preaching, many people who mount the pulpit appear to have abandoned long ago any attempt to expand their knowledge and understanding of theology. That is often the case with lay preachers, although the problem is not by any means limited to them. It is almost as if, having qualified to preach, those concerned regard further reading and study as unnecessary. They are like the athlete who, having won a race, decides to rest on his laurels rather than strive for higher performance.

If the churches were to introduce annual testing of all its active preachers to evaluate their acquaintance with, and understanding of, the latest biblical scholarship, it would be like asking backbench MPs to give a detailed explanation of the budget. An MP friend of mine once said at budget time: 'Don't ask me to explain it. All I have to do is be there when the division bell rings to vote for it.'

Some preachers substitute piracy for scholarship; they lift passages from books and articles and incorporate them in their sermons. A pirate preacher is usually easy to identify, being always closely attached to a manuscript and using language clearly not his or her own. University tutors across the disciplines are expert at identifying students with piratical tendencies, not least because they are familiar with all the books from which passages may be lifted to pad out essays. The ability to say what needs to be said in one's own words is a mark of the true scholar. It is also the mark of a true preacher. What we cannot explain from the pulpit in words that come from our own minds and hearts is in fact beyond the reach of our own understanding, so we shouldn't be offering it to others.

Of course, different congregations of Christians have different needs and capabilities. The level of scholarship required to address a gathering of the illustrious Society for Old Testament Study, admission to which requires a knowledge of Hebrew, is very different from that required to preach to the folk at a little old country chapel. In order to help hearers to grow spiritually in the way they need to do in the particular situations in which they find themselves, the intellectual demands upon worshippers must take account of their condition.

In 1744, settlers in Virginia built a college at Williamsburg. Having established good relations with the local Indians, they made an offer to educate six of their young men at the college. The response from the Indians was this:

> We know that you highly esteem the kind of learning taught in your colleges, and that the maintenance of our young men, while with you, would be very expensive to you. We are convinced, therefore, that you mean to do us good by your proposal and we thank you heartily.

> But you, who are wise, must know that different nations have different conceptions of things, and you will not take it amiss if our ideas of this kind of education happen not to be the same as yours.   We have had some experience of it; several of our young people were formerly brought up at the colleges of the northern provinces; they were instructed in all your sciences; but, when they came back to us, they were bad runners, ignorant of every means of living in the woods, unable to bear either cold or hunger, knew neither how to build a cabin, take a deer, nor kill an enemy, spoke our language imperfectly, were therefore neither fit for hunters, warriors nor counsellors;   they were totally good for nothing.

> We thank you for your kind offer, though we decline accepting it, and to show our grateful sense of it, if the gentlemen of Virginia will send us a dozen of their sons, we will take care of their education, instruct them in all we know, and make men of them.[8]

That brilliant encapsulation of the differences between races has relevance to all kinds of situations, including those facing preachers as they go about the world. Different people need different levels of theological understanding offered to them, to meet their needs in the lives they actually live day by day. The best scholar-preacher is able to handle that because his or her understanding is sufficient to be expressed in both simple and complex terms. To be profound with simplicity is a mark of the greatest scholar-preachers.

The Axe-Grinder

Richard Whately, Archbishop of Dublin in the middle of the nineteenth century, advised newcomers to the priesthood: 'Preach not because you have to say something, but because you have something to say.' Like much good advice, that is open to misunderstanding. While preachers, like lawyers and teachers, are rarely lost for something to say on any subject, using the pulpit to advance one's personal opinions on contentious issues creates disunity in the congregation. The letter to the Ephesians urges mutual forbearance among Christians for the maintenance of peace and unity. That requires the preacher to practise moderation in using the sermon as a vehicle for advancing a particular political, economic or social agenda. Of course, the gospel has implications in all those areas, but the preacher who appears to believe that there is only one legitimate Christian view in any one of them misleads and divides those who listen.

In his 'Ode Upon Cromwell's Return from Ireland', Andrew Marvell (1621-78) wrote of Charles I, as he mounted the scaffold:

He nothing common did or mean.
Upon that memorable scene,
But with his keener eye,
The axe's edge did try.

Keenly eyeing the preacher's blade, congregations faced with an axe-grinder know that any opinions they hold not consistent with those of the occupant of the pulpit will be quickly decapitated.

Of course, there have been those who could get away with being axe-grinder preachers by a combination of eloquence, good humour and, most important of all, a remarkable ability to convey a sense of personal humility. They eschew that kind of axe-grinding that has to do with achieving personal ends or settling old scores, which features widely in the commercial world, and a good many other places too. One outstanding exponent of what might be called the acceptable face of axe-grinding was Donald Soper. He was loved and respected by hearers of all persuasions, notwithstanding his apparent conviction that the kingdom of God above the bright blue sky was almost certainly bedecked with bright red flags.

Another greatly honoured axe-grinder was Martin Luther King. Few would question the way in which he related the gospel to the struggle for freedom of the black people of America.

Its most powerful expression came in a sermon entitled 'The American Dream'. It had its origins at the Lincoln Monument in Washington on American Independence Day 1963, at one of the greatest civil rights rallies in history. On that day, Martin Luther King gave to the world four words, passionately repeated over and over again: 'I have a dream.' Exactly two years later, King developed that message in a sermon at the Baptist Church in Atlanta of which he was pastor. It stands as a supreme example of a call for political and social change expressed in scriptural terms:

> I tell you this morning once more that I haven't lost faith. I still have a dream that one day all God's black children will be respected like his white children. I still have a dream this morning that one day the lion and the lamb will lie down together, and every man will sit under his own vine and fig tree, and none shall be afraid. I still have a dream this morning that one day all men everywhere will recognise that out of one blood God made all men to dwell upon the face of the earth. I still have a dream this morning that one day every valley will be exalted, and every mountain and hill made low; the rough places will be made plain, and the crooked places straight; and the glory of the Lord shall be revealed, and all flesh shall see it together. I still have a dream this morning that truth will reign supreme and all of God's children will respect the dignity and worth of human personality. And when this day comes, the morning stars will sing together and the sons of God will shout for joy.[9]

It is not possible to separate Martin Luther King's power as a preacher from the huge dimensions of the cause he pursued. It was one he was prepared to die for, and did. He gave the pursuit of political change from the pulpit not just respectability but a degree of compulsion. For the preacher to fail to speak out against evil in its political and social manifestations constitutes a loss of nerve and an abdication of responsibility.

But where does one draw the line? At what point does preaching about the political and social implications of the gospel go beyond what is acceptable? Many preachers have difficulty knowing the answer, as do some of the Specially Chosen Ones invited to deliver *Thought for the Day* on the radio. During the great miners' dispute of the l980s, the arrest of Arthur Scargill, the leader of the National Union of Miners (NUM), was likened by one such to the arrest of Jesus in the Garden of Gethsemane. In the attempt to span the gap between the Bible and current political and social issues, that surely went a bridge too far. The trouble with axe-grinding is that we all think it quite proper to grind our own axes, but have grave reservations about others who grind theirs. That is as true in the pulpit as anywhere else.

There is a sense in which preaching is by its nature an axe-grinding activity. We preach in order to convert others to our belief in the gospel, to sustain their faith thereafter and to provide guidance along the sometimes safe, sometimes treacherous road of life. The gospel we offer is unequivocal in the demands it makes upon those who seek to live by it. It requires abandonment of material values and commitment to service. The sharp axe of the gospel cuts down belief in the accumulation of wealth, thereby challenging the very basis upon which contemporary Western society operates. Far more powerful than any church assembly, be it ever so full of ecclesiastical dignitaries and theological experts, is any G8 gathering. When representatives of the world's eight richest nations meet, their decisions are waited upon with greater apprehension than the utterances of the General Synod of the Church of England, or the Methodist Conference, or the Assembly of the United Reformed Church, or the Evangelical Alliance, or the Pope. The preacher's insistence that placing one's faith in materialism brings not happiness and peace of mind but disaster is not a welcome message, but grinding that axe is a duty that cannot be avoided.

Is it possible to identify guidelines for preachers about how to relate the gospel to contemporary issues, and how not to do so? Three principles seem to the present writer to lie at the heart of getting it right, namely humility, breadth and an admission that we all see through a glass darkly. The least worthy form of pulpit axe-grinding is dogmatic, narrow and all-knowing.

The principal characteristic of those who go astray is their lack of humility. When a preacher has a bee in his or her bonnet about a particular interpretation of scripture, or a specific approach to protecting the environment, or a personal conviction about the extent of racial prejudice in Britain today, one is unlikely to hear any admission that there might be another view than their own. They are mistaken. There are many interpretations of scripture. How best to protect God's creation in the natural world is a highly complex issue. For example, while there seems to be an unarguable case for preserving the rain forests of South America, what are the implications of doing so at the expense of building a road through them that will bring economic prosperity to the poor of Central America? As for racism, repeated assertions by those with access to the media that our society is riven with institutional racism does not make it true, and a preacher who happens to believe it has no right to assume or insist that it is so to a congregation that cannot answer back; nor, of course, does someone who personally rejects all assertions that racism exists have the right to ram that message home to a body of worshippers. The axe-grinder's lack of humility, and unreadiness to accept that he or she just *might* be less than absolutely right, turns some worshippers right off.

The axe-grinder's second possible weakness is narrowness. There was a preacher so totally committed to the view that gambling was an unmitigated evil that he wove it into almost every sermon he preached. Doubtless he was influenced by the fact that his own childhood had been deeply unhappy because his father's wages were devoted to supporting his bookie rather than his family. The impoverished home was a battlefield. There is, of course, nothing wrong with challenging the moral efficacy of gambling. It is thoroughly consistent with questioning the materialism of our day and age. More people place their faith in winning the national lottery than in the gospel of Jesus. Three attitudes dominate the affluent nations in this day and age: faith, hope and rapacity. There is a widespread faith in material wealth, limitless hope of acquiring more and rapacious pursuit of that objective. It is impossible for the preacher to over-emphasise the contrast between those values and the teaching of Jesus. But there is a world of difference between presenting the gospel challenge to materialism and persistently focusing on one aspect of the acquisitive society as a result of one's personal experience and predilections. Congregations quickly realise that they are not hearing the whole gospel, in all its amazing breadth and depth, but a personal axe-grind. Listening to such preachers, one sometimes wonders whether they need not so much a pulpit as a psychiatrist.

The third weakness of the axe-grinder is his or her apparent belief that all has already been made clear by God on a preoccupying issue. The mantra of those who so believe often begins with the fatal phrase: 'I don't see how anyone can call themselves a Christian if they don't believe . . .' The sentence is completed by reference to the personal creed of the preacher in the field of Christian doctrine, or social priorities or, may the saints preserve us, political philosophy. It is my personal view that the saints do observe our goings-on, and maybe attempt to preserve us from the outcomes of our follies, but that is a highly personal view and insisting that others believe it would be quite out of order. We see through a glass darkly.

The axe-grinder most likely to hold a congregation, and to have his or her personal preoccupation lovingly tolerated, is the one who is careful to avoid dogmatism, to ensure that treatment of the issue about which he or she feels so strongly is subsumed in a presentation of the whole gospel, and to acknowledge that everyone's understanding of the things of God is slight compared with the truth that will one day be revealed. That is a tall order and, with the exception of what has already been said to justify it, axe-grinding in the pulpit is best avoided because it is so easily seen as having to do with the pursuit of personal power. An eminent Methodist academic lost no opportunity of attacking from the pulpit the emergence of numerous new translations of the Bible. He was particularly critical of colloquial versions which failed to be sufficiently faithful to the original Greek and Hebrew. 'I am,' he once announced in a sermon, 'conducting a personal campaign to put a stop to this sort of thing. I hope you are all with me.' Of course, a good many of his hearers were not. What's more, they knew they were not hearing a preacher who was offering a gospel message but someone playing in a power game.

The grinding of ecclesiastical axes requires special mention, not least because it is fairly common for the pulpit to be used as a place for addressing issues to do with church politics. The ordination of women and homosexuals, the preservation or abandonment of traditional models of ordained ministry, issues to do with church unity, are all areas of concern that have crept into the sermons of those who are not sure they should mention them, and erupted in the preaching of those who are quite sure they should.

What should we preachers have in mind when deciding if and how to address such issues as those mentioned? The most important consideration is surely that God intends us all to move forward in faith rather than dig ourselves in at whatever point we happen to have reached in our individual pilgrimages. We may feel safer in a doctrinal ditch than in the open territory ahead, but our God is a God of change and progress, not a God of the *status quo*. He sent Abraham out into the unknown and does the same with us. That being so, every issue must be addressed in terms of whether change seems to be in accordance with God's will. Not, be it noted, in terms of whether it accords with our personal wishes; not with regard to the impact on the worshipping community to which we happen to belong; not taking account of the personal satisfaction or discomfiture a particular development may bring. In a synod debate on church unity, a member was heard to say: 'It may be God's will but it's not *mine*.' He said he was only joking but more folk actually think that way than are prepared to admit it. The preacher must suppress any desire to advocate change, or to resist it, just because it happens to suit his or her personal circumstances and predilections. The advantage we preachers have in being able to express ourselves from the pulpit without fear of contradiction is one that we abuse at our peril.

In T S Eliot's *Murder in the Cathedral*, Archbishop Thomas Becket is tempted to welcome assassination as a route by which his name might live on as that of a glorious martyr. He says to himself that here would lie 'the greatest treason: to do the right deed for the wrong reason'. A temptation of the same kind faces any preacher in addressing an issue – social, political or ecclesiastical – about which he or she has an axe to grind. Here is a question for every preacher who, in preparing a sermon, is tempted to grind an axe: 'Why am I doing this?' If the right motive is in the heart, the right words will be on the lips.

There is something of the searcher in every preacher; something of the scholar; something of the axe-grinder. Sermon preparation may be affected by any number of influences, including the lectionary theme, the latest news on radio and television, the state of play in church politics and the kind of book the preacher happens to have been reading. Whatever happens to be exciting the mind or affecting the emotions of a preacher as a sermon is being planned will play a part in what he or she prepares to say to a congregation.

A minister who has been counselling a church member going through a crisis of faith may well preach a sermon about his or her own struggles as a searcher. Anyone who has been wrestling with one of those tough books of biblical scholarship, in which the academic footnotes on a page exceed the main text, is likely to enter the preacher-scholar mode. The man or woman who has an axe to grind about the way the voting went at synod after a debate on some issue to raise the passions will very likely carry his or her axe into the pulpit.

Less mighty matters also determine the preacher's mood and mode. It was widely recognised in one church that the young curate's sermons were powerfully affected by the behaviour of his four unruly children, who would rarely leave him in peace and drove him and his wife to distraction. The conditions under which he prepared what he would say in the pulpit or, as was often the case, failed to prepare because of domestic chaos, was a cause of some amusement to worshippers. On a good day, the verdict among them would be: 'He's had a quiet week at home, then!' Unsurprisingly, the curate was known to have particularly strong views on the breakdown of discipline in society and was a powerful axe-grinder on that subject.

That which most powerfully determines a preacher's style will be the condition of his or her belief, which will be affected by many passing influences and events. But for the searcher, the scholar, the axe-grinder, and all the other kinds of preacher one might name, the changelessness of God will be a hiding place from the winds of circumstance; it will be like the shadow of a great rock in a weary land. Provided the preacher's belief in God remains secure, his or her style of preaching will not matter very much. The French have a proverb: 'It is believing in roses that brings them to bloom.' It is the preacher's belief in the Lord that brings sermons to flower.

5

WHAT DOES THE CONGREGATION HAVE IN MIND?

The French philosopher Jean-Paul Sartre once observed: 'What I think makes me what I am. I can't prevent myself from thinking.'[1] So what do the members of today's church congregations have in mind, severally and collectively, when they gather for worship? What are they likely to be thinking about? The answer to that must inform the preacher's preparation.

For a start, they are far better acquainted with what is happening in the world at large than their forbears. Given the extent and sophistication of the modern communications media, people no longer have to imagine the impact of drought or civil war on the starving millions of Africa; the devastation and bloodshed brought to a city centre by a terrorist bomb; the expression on the face of a politician caught in some sexual indiscretion. The preacher addresses a congregation for whom what is happening in the world is proximate to worship rather than remote from it. They come with the latest disaster buzzing in their minds.

The proximity of national and international events to the lives of ordinary people offers the preacher an opportunity to interpret the world to a congregation in relation to the gospel. But there is a danger here. In analysing the work of all whose careers lie in portraying events, the novelist Martin Bedford has rightly observed that, every time we write down or otherwise record our version of events, we take one step back from the truth. [2] The task facing the preacher in interpreting the world to a modern congregation is that of holding fast to the message that Jesus is the truth rather than, as mentioned before, giving flight to his or her own opinions on political, economic and social issues. That is not easy and handling it requires a degree of humility some of us find it hard to summon up.

In my first ministerial appointment, at an inner city mission, I found myself working with a man with very strong political views on the other side of the party divide from mine. He was one of the most caring and devoted servants of the Lord I have ever met: the nearest thing to a saint I am likely to meet this side of eternity. But his politics created a problem for me, not least because he seemed unable to appreciate that any Christian could possibly think otherwise than he did, and frequently made that clear from the pulpit. My reaction was to respond to his assertions by presenting the other side of the argument when it was my turn to preach. He soon realised what I was up to and got into the habit of saying, after making a political point in a sermon, 'Peter will no doubt answer me when he is up here next week.' Interestingly, we had a splendid working relationship and the congregation regarded our rather Socratic method of debate with great amusement. Worshippers understand the temptation that comes to all preachers when some recent event in the news offers them a golden opportunity to air their personal prejudices, carefully couched, of course, in some seemingly appropriate biblical text. The amazing tolerance of church folk is only stretched beyond its limit if a preacher persists in politicising the pulpit and turning services into holy hustings.

But the preacher's personal prejudices have far less impact than one might fear because not everybody will be listening. In the eighteenth century, when the great Restoration playwrights turned playgoing into one of the most flourishing activities of the leisured classes, the play to be shown became a secondary consideration. In her novel *Evelina*, Fanny Burney (1752-1840) has a revealing exchange between two characters. 'Do you come to the play,' asks one, 'without knowing what it is?' This brings the response, 'O yes sir, yes, very frequently. I have no time to read playbills. One merely comes to meet one's friends, and show that one's alive.' Now that so many churchgoers have been about for more than three score years and ten, it's perhaps not surprising that they sometimes seem to attend worship primarily to register their continued existence, and swop survival stories with their contemporaries.

A feature of all congregations is the variety of experiences contained in them and affecting the thinking of individuals. All of life is probably right there in front of the preacher. There are few if any tales of life's agonies or ecstasies one can use as pulpit illustrations which will not bring the response, 'I've been there', from at least one worshipper. In his poem 'Metamorphoses', Yevgeny Yevtushenko draws this picture of life's pattern:

> Childhood is the village of Rosycheekly,
> Little Silly, Clamberingoverham,
> Leapfrogmorton, going towards Cruelidge,
> Through Unmaliciousness and Clearvisiondon.
>
> Youth is the village of Hopeworth,
> Expansiongrove, Seducehall,
> And, well, if it's a bit like Foolmouth,
> All the same it is Promising.
>
> Maturity is the village of Divideways,
> Either Involvementhaven or Hidewell,
> Either Cowardsbridge or Bravewater,
> Either Crookedwood or Justfield.
>
> Old age is the village of Tiredhead,
> Understandmore, Little Reproach,
> Forgetfast, Overgrownend,
> And, God keep us from it, Lonelybury.[3]

'Lonelybury' is a land all people inhabit from time to time, and not only in old age. All who come to worship experience, from time to time, feelings of separation from others, and from God. It is a universal state of mind and heart and soul. Only the gospel has the answer to that problem. Every time it is preached, the issue of loneliness is addressed.

But more superficial issues are also likely to occupy worshippers' minds some of the time. The Lord's sheep come to church bringing their tales behind them – accounts of the latest triumph by the home team at the local football stadium, or the latest disaster; stories about what it's rumoured the girls got up to with the boys at the youth club disco; analysis of Mrs Hobson's latest operation, with euphemistic references to unmentionable organs; reviews of the local council's poor performance in emptying wheeliebins, or repairing the roads, or preventing vandalism by those teenage louts who wouldn't have been allowed to get away with it in my day. The hubbub that fills some churches before worship begins to make Question Time in the House of Commons seem quite orderly. Ralph Waldo Emerson wrote in an essay entitled 'Self Reliance', in 1841, 'I like the silent church before the service begins better than any preaching.' That was more than a hundred and fifty years ago. Emerson would find it more difficult today to find a church where reflective silence is observed before worship.

In some churches today, preparation for worship by music groups has the effect of making quiet reflection impossible. While some such groups play quietly, engendering a reflective atmosphere, some do not. There are places where those now designated worship leaders exercise their ministry in the manner of an old time music hall. 'Come on, let's hear it for Jesus!' was the demand of one chord-crashing guitarist of a congregation not sufficiently inclined to join in the frolics which preceded the arrival of the preacher. Far from preparing people to worship, such an approach requires the preacher to change the mood to one of reverence before true worship can begin.

That is, of course, an exaggeration. In truth, there are many worshippers who need and prefer to make a joyful noise unto the Lord before worship. A church which cares for all its worshippers will try to keep a balance between those who yearn for the good old days when quietness was observed and those who wish to fill the church with singing before the preacher takes over proceedings.

Whatever is done, the outcome for the preacher will be that what the congregation has in mind before a service begins will be influenced by proceedings in church over which he or she has little control. The inconsistency between the theme of a service and what happens before it begins is sometimes remarkable. 'Come on and celebrate', with whooping and clapping, is perhaps not the best musical prelude to a preacher calling a congregation to worship by reciting the message of Isaiah 30:15: 'Thus said the Lord God, the Holy One of Israel . . . in quietness and trust shall be your strength.'

Not all who come to church have it in mind to listen to preaching. Any impact one has is slight. The attitude of my hairdresser to my words of wisdom provides an illustration. 'I heard you on the radio the other day,' he said, as he snipped away. I waited excitedly for him to relate whatever astute observation of mine had provided a brilliant insight into some eternal truth. 'Yes,' he said, 'but I can't remember what you were talking about.' One may take comfort in such situations from the thought that some seed may have been planted in the hearer's mind that will one day germinate. The preacher must press on with the task, even when he or she knows there are those with no mind to listen. The prophets of the Old Testament often addressed people whose minds were closed to their message and today's preacher stands in that mighty tradition.

Preaching being a means by which God's presence is evoked, in what kind of worship situation might that best be realised? Not all worshippers have the same answer in mind. In particular, there is a divide between those who have come to be known as traditionalists and those labelled charismatics. It is a false distinction but, since many Christians appear to see themselves as falling into one or other category, an understanding of it is essential for any preacher.

Possession of the divine charisma, the Spirit of the Lord, is a fundamental feature of the Judaeo-Christian tradition. When Saul was anointed by Samuel as Yahweh's chosen one to rule over Israel, he declared that the Spirit of the Lord would come upon him and he would be turned into another man (1 Samuel 10:6). As Bernhard Anderson so accurately perceives in his *Living World of the Old Testament*, Saul never showed any great understanding of the profounder aspects of Israel's faith but, believing that the Lord was at work in him, he went out fearlessly against Israel's enemies, whatever the odds.[4] He placed his trust in the charism, the Spirit of the Lord at work in him, which the *Oxford English Dictionary* defines quite simply as 'a favour specially vouchsafed by God, a grace, a talent'. That which was subsequently seen by Isaiah as being the characteristic by which the Messiah might in due course be identified was his possession of the charisma: the Spirit of the Lord would be upon him. In fulfilment of that prophecy, Jesus declared at Nazareth (Luke 4:l8): 'The Spirit of the Lord is upon me.' The charismatic nature of his ministry was made clear.

To the extent that all Christians believe the Holy Spirit to be at work in them, all are charismatics. But some believe themselves to be more possessed by the Spirit than others; more influenced in their lives by the gifts the Spirit bestows; closer than other Christians to the actual source of power that comes from being filled with the Holy Spirit, as the first disciples were at Pentecost. The question often asked by charismatics of others is: 'Are you Spirit-filled?' By implication, if you are not sufficiently sure of the Spirit's power in your life, and able to demonstrate it, you are a tea bag short of a Christian cup of tea. Worshippers of traditional and less excitable disposition sometimes find all this at best embarrassing and at worst objectionable.

Within many congregations, there are believers of both kinds, and none-too-choosy folk who are happy to go along with whatever worship style a preacher adopts. The one essential in the situation facing the church today is this: that anyone appointed to lead worship in a particular place discovers the theological complexion of the congregation, and has regard to it.

How a preacher handles it will, of course, depend in part on his or her own theological position. But that ought not to be the principal determinant of what is done. The preacher's duty when addressing a theologically mixed congregation is to ensure that the sermon embraces those of all persuasions. The structure of the service should support that purpose. An important duty of the referee at a football match has been defined by the Football Association as being to ensure that, as far as possible, whatever conflicts may occur on the field, the game flows smoothly. The preacher must similarly ensure that, whatever conflicts of opinion about how best to worship God there are in a congregation, a coherent experience is provided embracing everyone in which everything flows smoothly together. That is no easy task, but it is being done and must be done because, for want of it, some of the Lord's sheep will look up, find that they are not being fed, and not come again. The unhappy division of whole churches into traditional ones and those identified as charismatic is the result.

At a more mundane level, panic in the vestry is an all-too-frequent preliminary to worship, significantly affecting a congregation's mood and turn of mind. One of the commonest reasons for it is the now widespread availability of microphone facilities in churches. Unfortunately, training in their efficient use has trailed way behind their installation. A fairly typical situation is one where the church steward on duty at a service says, on being asked if there's a microphone, and whether or not it is switched on, 'We've got one, but I've no idea how it works. I don't think the chap who knows is here, but I'll go and look.'

A similarly unhelpful situation often faces a visiting preacher unfamiliar with what normally happens at a church. On being rung up and asked if the Sunday School will be coming in for the first part of a morning service, a church steward has been known to say, 'Yes, I *think* so.' The preacher, having carefully prepared something for the children, is told on arrival, 'Oh, no. The children never come in on this Sunday of the month.'

Economic historians have discovered a document which portrays the rules by which daily life was governed in an English village in the Middle Ages. The *Rectitudines Singularum Personarum*, or rules for each single person, identified the responsibilities of everyone from the humble villein upwards on a feudal manor. But the *Rectitudines* did not derive from any statute, despite their being applied with the force of law in the event of disputes: they were simply the committing to a manuscript of practices which had grown up over the centuries which all accepted. By ancient right and custom, manorial life was governed from the cradle to the grave. The class structure to which that situation gave rise only began to crumble when the economic system on which it depended began to collapse. With that collapse came a questioning of the social order famously expressed by John Ball in the fourteenth century, and still relevant today in a society where class remains a key to power:

> When Adam delved and Eve span,
> Who was then the gentleman?

That medieval diversion is provided to make a point. Just as manorial life was governed by the power of custom and practice, so is the life of most churches. Worshippers know what usually happens and, being themselves familiar with local practice, fail to realise what a visiting preacher needs to be told. What is more, church stewards too readily assume that what happens in *their* church is exactly the same as what happens in others. It is an assumption that rarely reflects reality. The narrow preoccupations that occupy the minds of some congregations also affect the quality of worship. A meeting of worshippers was held to discuss developments in church buildings and worship arrangements. It was entitled 'Changing Styles of Pulpit and Pew' and advance publicity identified questions that promised a fascinating debate about conditions in which preaching might most powerfully and effectively take place. In the event, by far the longest exchange at the meeting arose from the insistence of some of those present that churches ought to be more ready than they are to have modern hymns rather than traditional ones.

There was a time when the music in the minds of church folk was much the same everywhere. Choosing hymns for a service was a simple business. No more. It has become an exercise rather like choosing wallpaper: the number of alternatives has become mind-boggling. Discovering the different hymn books, song books, overhead transparencies and photocopied collections of this and that scattered round a group of churches in a parish or Methodist circuit requires the determination of a suspicious customs officer. What's more, one visit to preach at a church may lead someone to think they have cracked it when it turns out not to be so, seeing that places of worship are generating their own preferred anthologies at a speed that makes Michael Schumacher seem a bit of an old slowcoach. Again, of course, I exaggerate to make a point, but it is a very important one. Congregations sometimes seem to give little thought to the process by which a preacher prepares to lead worship, and the need for him or her to have accurate information about local custom and practice.

The place of children in the church presents another hazard for the preacher. Many worshippers struggle in their minds with being open and welcoming to children on the one hand and maintaining an atmosphere of quiet reflection as worship begins. 'Here come the storm troopers,' announced one church stalwart of mature years as the children arrived for their customary battle over who was going to sit where, and with whom. The development of all-age worship has in some places led to a good deal of mutual hostility in the congregation. 'They shouldn't be here if they can't behave', is an all too common comment about children in worship. It usually comes from those who belong to a generation brought up to believe that children should be seen and not heard.

What should a church do to acknowledge children in worship, and give them a properly honoured place, without allowing that to destroy the atmosphere for everyone else? There is now plenty of guidance available on the components of all-age worship but little on the subject of the conditions in which it should take place. A couple of rules emerge, like the *Rectitudines*, from successful practice.

Firstly, all those who are part of a worshipping community, young and old and in between, need to undertake a programme of training in what might be called mutual acceptance. It is not sufficient to assume that everyone will be happy together. Some churches have taken a great deal of trouble to re-educate worshippers with regard to the relationship between the generations in this day and age. Their example needs to be more widely adopted. What prevents that happening is the widespread conviction that everything's alright really, or will be if left to sort itself out. It will not sort itself out. 'I never come to church for family services,' said one elderly woman, 'the children are in and I can never hear a thing.' When some people stop worshipping because other people are going to be present, a church is in trouble.

Secondly, church councils and other such bodies must establish and publicise arrangements for ensuring that the presence of a noisy and disruptive child does not make a worshipful atmosphere impossible. Many of us have known the experience of having a crying child in church, or one running about, or a couple making a racket, and nobody does anything. A kindly word and helping hand from a steward can often relieve a parent of great embarrassment. There needs to be a place in every church to which children who are disrupting worship may be taken. Similar provision might also be appropriate for members of the retired ladies' club who chatter away in the back pew in between the hymns.

In a piece in the *Houston Telegraph*, written before he became famous, Abraham Lincoln was described as so ungainly, and his appearance so unattractive, that he was without hope of success as a leader. 'He has,' said the report, 'most unwarrantably abused the privilege, which all politicians have, of being ugly.' While it would be going too far to suggest that a preacher's physique affects the impact he or she makes, a congregation's mind may well be distracted, or otherwise affected, by the manner of dress adopted.

There was a time when the dress of ordained persons was designed to hide personal identity. The black cassock was, and remains, the clearest example. But today, what a preacher wears quite often constitutes a statement about his or her position on some issue, sometimes theological, sometimes social, sometimes political. For example, a green cassock may be used to indicate interest in green issues; support for environmental lobbyists; commitment to protecting the world's natural resources. Ordained ministers in nonconformist churches who decline to wear any vestments are usually anxious to exercise their low theological position, while those whose manner of dress in worship makes them look like priests of the established church may be anxious to make it known that they are moving up the theological scale. In a pamphlet he has written about liturgical dress, entitled *Blackbirds and Budgerigars*, Norman Wallwork writes that 'it is now possible to see a Methodist minister in a grey cassock, with bright blue tunnel shirt still showing above his bands, wearing a black gown, a green stole and a pectoral cross'. Norman's verdict is simple: 'The blackbird has been eaten by the budgerigar.' He also observes that the often impressive, highly individualistic garments donned by some ministers 'can carry only the liturgical significance invested in them by the wearer'.[5]

Ministers are not alone among preachers in devising vestmental fashions that make personal statements. A Methodist local preacher of my acquaintance who, in black suit, white shirt and academic gown and hood looks for all the world like a clergyman who has accidentally left his dog collar at home, has said quite openly that he wants to emphasise the status of lay persons in the pulpit, and their absolute equality with any ordained person in the preaching role.

A young man who was training to teach arrived at my school one morning to start teaching practice. He looked as if he had slept rough. His long hair was unkempt, his jeans and his jumper were filthy and his shoes had obviously never been cleaned. I told him to remove himself from the premises because his appearance disqualified him from being fit to stand in front of a class. I explained that, before uttering a word to young people, a teacher's first impact on a class was determined by his appearance. He would in effect be saying that sloppiness was acceptable, which would be taken to mean that standards in general didn't matter. As a teacher, he was a visual disaster.

Some preachers have a touch of disaster about their appearance. No matter if the church heating is not up to much, climbing the pulpit in an anorak is never justified, but it's been done. Thermal underwear is an essential basis for powerful preaching in unheated churches, even if the preacher's speciality is not the hot gospel.

But appearance amounts to more than manner of dress. A common weakness among newcomers to the pulpit, and some not so new, is the inclination to avoid eye-contact with the congregation. By contrast, the best preachers look the customers right in the eye, which is the gateway to the heart. Preaching to the ceiling at the back of the church never has the same effect.

The preacher's congregation is made up of all sorts and conditions of people, each one of whom has a unique story to tell. The task one faces in offering the gospel is that of feeding all the Lord's sheep, be they ever so diverse. It is in reality beyond human capability. But let not any newcomer to preaching be discouraged, or any old-stager who, after offering the gospel more times than he or she can remember, is wondering whether to continue as congregations decline. The good news is that we are called to be faithful, not successful. God will secure his purposes in his own way, and in his own good time. He it is who will ensure, with just a little bit of help from us, and a great deal of unseen activity on his part, that congregations hear the message he has in mind for each one of them.

In the heat of youthful ambition, I thought Rudyard Kipling's poem 'If' to be sentimental doggerel. Life has taught me otherwise. In particular, its reference to triumph and disaster as being two impostors we should treat the same powerfully reflects my experience. Certainly, a congregation will often have a higher regard for what we offer when we think we have failed, and a lower opinion of what we regard as our triumphs, than ever we imagine. Only the men and women in a preacher's congregation are aware of what the Lord has done for each of them in an act of worship.

One of a group of tourists being shown round the Art Gallery of Ontario in Toronto by a specialist in modern art inquired as to the meaning of a picture which appeared to be merely a confusion of brilliant brush strokes. 'A picture means,' the guide replied, 'whatever it means to you. What is it saying? Whatever you hear it saying to you.' The picture in words that the preacher paints will mean whatever God intends it to mean to the different members of a congregation, whatever they have on their minds.

6

AUTOLYCUS THE PREACHER

A woman sits at a table on which there is a pile of cannibalised newspapers. She wears a loose-fitting housecoat to which numerous cuttings from the papers are pinned. She unpins them and shuffles through the collection. Some she rejects; those remaining are set aside for her eldest surviving son. It is the early 1960s and the woman is Rose Fitzgerald Kennedy, who regularly supplies the President of the United States of America with material he might find useful.

Notwithstanding his having aides galore, President Kennedy was known to make use of material supplied by his mother. There is a story that the brilliant sound bite that made his visit to Berlin before the Wall came down such a triumph was suggested by her. 'All free men,' he said, 'wherever they may live, are citizens of Berlin. And therefore, as a free man, I take pride in the words *Ich bin ein Berliner.*' Some say Rose Kennedy got the idea from her record of Churchill's speech in America during the war when, desperate to bring about an alliance against the Nazi terror, he simply asked, 'What sort of people do they think we are?' It's called identifying with your audience, and getting them to identify with you. Churchill and Kennedy were both masters of that art. In Kennedy's case, his mastery seems to have been achieved with just a little bit of help from mum.

Jack was not always grateful for his mother's contributions to his national leadership.[1] She once had a notion to get him and the Russian leader to sign some photographs of themselves together. As a first step, she sent them to Krushchev for his signature, then passed them to the White House for the President to sign. She received this response:

> Dear Mother,
>
> If you are going to contact the heads of state, it might be a good idea to consult me or the State Department first, as your gesture might lead to international complications.
>
> Love, Jack

She replied, insisting none too seriously:

> Dear Jack,
>
> I am so glad you warned me about contacting the heads of state, as I was just about to write to Castro.
>
> Love, Mother

Rose Fitzgerald Kennedy was all her life a collector of interesting material from all kinds of sources, and a recorder of any immediate thoughts that might one day prove useful. A preacher needs to follow that same practice. Nothing is more annoying than to find, in preparing a sermon, that one has read or heard something somewhere or other that would have provided just the right illustration to drive a point home, but the place to find it just cannot be called to mind. Like Autolycus in Shakespeare's *The Winter's Tale*, we preachers must be snappers-up of unconsidered trifles.

Asked why his sermons were filled with illustrations, William Sangster replied that they served as lampposts along the road of understanding, lighting up what might otherwise be only dimly understood. In fact, the sermon illustration serves at least three purposes: to secure the congregation's attention, to illuminate ideas and to relate the gospel to the ordinary experiences of daily life.

Creating a Listening Congregation

The first task of a preacher is to secure and hold the attention of the congregation. That is a statement of the obvious, but its fundamental importance is not always appreciated. The notion that worshippers ought to listen is one we all fall into from time to time. But to assume that everybody has come to church in order to give rapt attention to the preacher's every word shows the misplaced confidence one has when starting a crossword in ink. The attentive congregation is created, not ready-made. One way of getting people to listen is by the strategic use of illustrations, to which end the preacher needs a store of material. But two words of caution are needed as to its use.

First, not every illustration will connect with everyone. What is a turn-on for some may be a turn-off for others. While a reference to football may make some prick up their ears, it may well cause others to groan with despair. Similarly, assuming that everyone is familiar with the latest episode of *EastEnders* can be fatal; some folk are engrossed in its every story-line but others have no idea what it's all about, nor any wish to be informed. That's not an argument against using material from such sources, but one must paint one's pictures in a variety of colours.

The second word of caution follows from the first. The preacher must be careful to diversify his or her illustrations. Regularly drawing them from one area of life may well prove more boring than using none at all. A ministerial colleague who has retired to the Isle of Man tells me that the island is full of wenize: wealthy retired folk who, after lives of service in what once used to be called the colonies, endlessly tell tales beginning, 'When I was in Kenya . . .' or wherever. There are a few preachers about who have wenize tendencies.

Of course, the creation of a listening congregation is not exclusively the responsibility of the preacher. Those who come to hear a sermon have three duties. The first is to come prepared, the second is to be expectant and the third is to approach in humility. There is no room to develop those three important concepts in this book, but they are set down here as a reminder that what the Lord may achieve through the words of preachers depends not only upon those who have been raised up to proclaim the gospel but also upon those who listen, or fail to do so.

As a means of encouraging people to listen, an illustration operates in two ways. It may lay the trail to a critical proposition, or it may operate as a resting place in the course of a sermon.

Here is an example of a story snapped up and used to secure attention at the start of a sermon about our dependence on God rather than our own cleverness:

> Jimmy's mother took him to the doctor. 'Doctor,' she said, 'can a boy perform an appendix operation on himself?' 'Of course not,' replied the doctor. 'See,' said the mother, turning to her son, 'now put it back.'

Yes, it's just a simple joke, but the use to which it may be put is quite profound. Many of the greatest disasters in history have occurred because someone has tried to remove their own appendix. Time and again, leaders have arisen who have placed their confidence in their own ambition and power; trusted in their own cleverness; failed to acknowledge the supremacy of God. How easily the story of Jimmy leads into that mighty proposition. Thus may a sermon that begins with a smile end in tears of repentance.

The first great exponent of the humorous illustration as a means of securing attention at the start of a sermon was John Donne. In 1623, Shakespeare's play *Much Ado About Nothing* had audiences falling about at the Globe Theatre, principally because of comments by Beatrice, the leading female character, about the stupidity of men. A favourite was her withering observation that marriage was something for a woman to avoid since it might well mean her being forced to live with 'a clod of wayward marl'. Mounting the pulpit at St Paul's during the play's run, Donne began:

> In the great ant hill of the whole world, I am
> an ant. In the great field of clay, of red earth,
> that man was made of, I am a *clod*.[2]

Everyone present knew that Donne was using the knockabout stuff down at the Globe as a way of getting their attention. He then launched into an account of human cloddishness in failing to acknowledge God. There is a story that, as Donne left the cathedral that day, one noble gentleman was heard to say, 'He calls not only himself an ant and a clod, but me as well, I like it not.' Donne knew how to make his hearers smile, then realise they were smiling at their own peculiarities and weaknesses, or maybe refusing to smile because the preacher's message had struck too deep for laughter.

On my arrival in Newcastle some years ago, it was swarming with young people heading for St James's Park to hear Bruce Springsteen, who was flying in from America with his band. My own business in the city had to do with the great teachers' pay dispute of the 1980s and the BBC sent a camera crew along to my hotel to do a short piece for the local evening news programme. The girls behind reception were enormously impressed to have someone staying who was going to be on the telly. 'Excuse me, sir,' said one, 'but are you one of Bruce Springsteen's roadies?'

Being mistaken for what we are not can leave us speechless. Not being recognised for what we are can have more serious implications. When the people around us are unaware of our identity as practising Christians – as

Jesus Roadies – we fail the Lord. My Newcastle experience has provided me with a trail along which worshippers may be taken to consider that important question. Any experience a preacher has had which bears upon his or her identity may be used in the same way.

An illustration may also operate as a sermon's resting place. A congregation considering some profound theological question needs a break. A preacher travelling down the road of God's omnipotence may well find that hearers need a short rest in a lay-by on the way. My wife's ability to know when my hand is poised over the car keys on the hall table at home, when it would be best for me to exercise my legs to get to the village post office, has given worshippers a moment's respite. 'Why don't you walk?' my all-seeing wife calls from some distant part of the house. Getting back on the road of God's all-seeing power from that anecdotal lay-by was not far to travel. A preacher's domestic adventures are a source of endless interest to worshippers and will often supply the relief illustration a sermon may need.

Illuminating the Message

There are not many interpretations of the gospel that cannot be made clearer and driven home by the use of an appropriate illustration. Theological generalisations without explanation do little to advance people's understanding; explanations without illustration do not take matters much further. In seeking out ways of making plain the gospel's meaning by reference to stories and exemplifications, preachers explore and extend their own understanding. Here is a question for all newcomers to preaching to consider: if you can't illustrate what you mean, are you sure you fully understand it yourself? Some experienced pulpit performers need to think about that too.

Let's take one of the most difficult subjects a preacher has to handle: the Trinity. A preacher wrote to a national newspaper to say that going to a test match had given him the perfect illustration for a sermon on the doctrine of the Trinity. The last three balls he watched were bowled by England's new spin bowler. The first was a leg-spinner, the second a top-spinner and the third a googly. There it was: one person expressing himself in three different but very similar ways. The leg-spinner's stock ball represents God the Father, who created us to feel after him; the top-spinner, which goes straight through, represents the direct activity of God the Son; the googly represents the surprising activity of God the Holy Spirit. Doubtless a number of alert preachers snapped up that illuminating analogy.[3]

Autolycus the preacher must be constantly adding to his or her collection of illustrative bric-a-brac; always alert to the possibility that something useful may turn up. There was a poster on the wall in the baby unit of a large London hospital which advised trainee nurses: *The First Five Minutes of Life are Dangerous.* Someone had added underneath: *The Last Five Minutes are Pretty Dodgy Too!* That simple illustration of the fears we all have of old age and death provides a good basis for exploring some aspects of eschatology: a subject which is not everyone's cup of tea.

Newspapers regularly provide a rich source of illustrative material, not least in their letters columns. Take, for example, this one written to *The Times:*

Sir,

As if the human race has not enough troubles to bedevil it, we make things worse by continuing to warn each other of the fatal consequences of our everyday habits. Smoking gives us cancer; butter clogs our arteries; eggs ruin our livers; sweets rot our teeth; coffee gives us insomnia; brandy brings on heart attacks; sex drives us mad; more sex drives us madder, and so on. Could we not rationalise the situation into one all-embracing statement: Just Living Kills You In The End?

A government health warning to that effect could be made to appear, by law, on all birth certificates.

Yours faithfully,
Monja Danischewsky [4]

The impact of those words is the greater when it is made known to a congregation that they appeared a quarter of a century ago. Since then, further dangers have been discovered to alarm us in the things we eat and drink. Preoccupation with the physical grows apace, while human spirituality is neglected. The letter provides a good example of something snapped up long ago that has grown more valuable as a resource over the years. Autolycus the preacher should be reluctant to throw anything away.

One's illustrations do not necessarily have to be of today, but they must have application here and now. Back in 1274, Peter the Hermit wrote these words:

> The world is passing through troubled times. Young people today think of nothing but themselves. They have no reverence for parents or old people. They are impatient of all restraint. They talk as if they alone know everything and what passes for wisdom in us is foolishness to them. As for the girls, they are forward, immodest and unworthy in speech, behaviour and dress. [5]

Those words have given much comfort to parents who have come to church worrying about the problems they are having with their teenage offspring. Conflicts between the generations go back beyond the Norman Conquest to the very beginning of civilization, but it's no good just telling people that: they need the reassurance that comes from a piece of evidence. Autolycus the preacher is *inter alia* an evidence-gatherer.

The Gospel and Everyday Life

Folk come to church on Sunday for help and guidance in facing life on Monday morning. They come for other reasons too, and the preacher has a more far-reaching duty than simply to equip folk to face the week ahead, but unless a sermon does that, it will fall short of the purpose God intends. That being so, illustrations which reflect and impact upon daily life as one's hearers experience it should be a key feature of a preacher's collection.

The everyday life illustration aims to evoke the response: 'Yes, yes, of course, it's true. I've been there.' That response is not only sought in church: authors and playwrights also strive for it. When John Osborne's *Look Back in Anger* was first staged in the l950s, it took England by storm precisely because young people of a new generation heard the leading character express what *they* felt about the condition of society. Despite its title, there was no looking back after Jimmy Porter raved about the distorted values of a world that was passing away. We who were young at the time knew that a new era was coming to birth. The preacher's task is to evoke a similar response so that people say: 'Yes, it must be so. What we hear is what we say in our hearts.'

There was a queue at a station buffet in which a young man with a backpack was carefully counting the change in his hand. Reaching the counter, he asked for a coffee. 'Large or small?' said the young girl who was serving. Looking at the coins he was holding, the backpacker asked, 'What's the difference?' The girl replied, 'With large, you get more coffee.' That example of the funny things you hear as you go about this world – a phenomenon with which all worshippers are familiar in their own experience – provides a good sermon illustration of how we human beings fail to communicate even at the simplest level. The consequences in the home, in the church and in our relationship with God can be dire. On hearing that proposition, the worshipper will surely say, 'Yes, it is so. I know in my heart it is true.' Autolycus the preacher should always be alert to what people around are saying: a rich seam of illustrations may be mined by listening to the conversations one hears. That being a favourite activity of mine, it is perhaps no wonder that a common observation in churches which have been my responsibility has been, 'You want to watch out what you say when he's around. He writes it all down, you know.'

A good everyday illustration from the lazy, hazy days of summer may be found in Francis Clifford's novel, *The Naked Runner.*[6] Here is an arresting passage to focus a congregation's thinking when the bees are buzzing round in their gardens at home:

> According to the theory of aerodynamics, and as may be readily demonstrated by means of a wind tunnel, the bumble bee is unable to fly. That is because the size, weight and shape of his body in relation to the total wing span make flight impossible. But the bumble bee, being ignorant of these scientific facts, and possessing considerable determination, does fly – and makes a little honey too.

The only time a sermon of mine has been heckled was when that passage was quoted. 'Rubbish!' shouted a man in the congregation, on hearing the first two sentences. But he changed his mind after hearing the conclusion. 'Yes, yes, yes!' he exclaimed. But there's a bigger yes in Francis Clifford's words than one just for the bees. If we have enough determination in walking in God's way, we will take off too. Told this, my interrupter got up, turned to address the congregation and said, 'It's true, you know.' His final yes was the response we preachers seek from all those to whom we preach. A good illustration is more likely to evoke it than a multitude of elaborate theological assertions.

Preachers must snap up whatever happens to pass before their eyes or come to their ears, or feature in their experience, *at the time.* It is no good searching back in books or newspapers one has read – even if they happen still to be available – or to go delving into one's memory of events at the moment when the need arises to illustrate or hammer home a message. Building up a bank of material is the name of the preacher's game. A squirrel does not wait for winter to search for nuts. Many a preacher has faced a sermonic winter of discontent through not having established a fat file of bits and pieces. Three factors should be borne in mind in building one up.

Firstly, what any preacher snaps up will very likely turn out to serve several purposes. The same story or quotation may be used for any of the three identified: to rivet a congregation's attention, to illuminate, or to relate what is being said to everyday life. Lindsay Dawn Low's letter to a national newspaper at Christmas thirty years ago has served all those purposes. But when it was first snapped up there was no thought of how it might be used. Its impact on me was so great that there was no doubting its effect on others, however deployed:

> Dear Santa,
>
> Will you bring me a pram for my dolly and my big brother safe from Ireland please.
>
> Love from
>   Lindsay Dawn Low

Time, and the genuine prospect of peace in Northern Ireland, have not blunted the force of that letter, which illustrates many things: the simple trust of a child, the heartache and yearning that conflict brings, the concern for one another that lies within a family, the hope and expectation that all can be made well. Lindsay's few words are a sermon in themselves, are they not?

Secondly, constant alertness is the key to accumulating a good file. A successful snapper-up always has a notebook to hand when reading a book, listening to the radio or watching television; scissors to hand when reading the papers; a ready ear to record conversations; time to make a record of experiences.

Thirdly, the good snapper-up is sufficiently systematic to be able to find what he or she is looking for when need arises. It is not best practice to accumulate material in the same way that most of us have a drawer at home in which we toss things that might come in handy one day. When the moment comes that we want something from that drawer, having convinced ourselves that what we need is in there somewhere, we can never find it. Hell hath no fury like that of the husband scrabbling through a collection of old plugs, bits of string, nuts and bolts, elastic bands, broken screwdrivers and much else besides, unable to find that old padlock that used to be for Johnny's bike before he grew up, and would now be just the thing to make secure the new deed box bought, as retirement approaches, because of an urge to put all the family documents in good order.

Martin Luther King was a prime example of an autolycan preacher. In the introduction to *A Knock at Midnight*, a collection of his greatest sermons, one learns that he maintained 'a rich repertoire of quotations, stories and set pieces that could be called forth for any occasion'.[8] As his ministry developed, his collection increasingly featured stories from his own life, carefully recorded lest he forget them, and stories from the lives of his congregation. Nor was he averse to storing the sermons of other preachers and adapting them to his own style.

Autolycus, being as he put it 'littered under Mercury', the god of trickery, lived on his wits at the expense of simple and unsuspecting folk who were easily duped. The unconsidered trifles he snapped up were other people's possessions. But, as *The Winter's Tale* draws to a close, it becomes clear that some good has come out of Autolycus's trickery. 'Here come those,' he says of a couple of innocents who have come into a fortune through his actions, 'I have done good to against my will.' Not by accident but intent, we who occupy the pulpit bring good fortune to our hearers by using material we have snapped up to add power and penetration to our preaching.

7

PREACHING TODAY

When Peter stood and addressed the crowds gathered in Jerusalem at Pentecost and preached the *kerygma*, the story of God's salvation plan, he launched a programme of conversion on a world in which few doubted the existence of a deity, or deities. In due course, the West was largely converted to the gospel Peter proclaimed and what has come to be called the Christian era unfolded.

Today's preachers proclaim the gospel to a largely deconverted Western world: one which once believed but does no longer. Deconversion has not only come upon Western society at large, but is also widely evident within the church. An earlier chapter emphasised the biblical illiteracy of the average modern worshipper. The authority of the Bible, or its lack of it, is the subject of endless argument among scholars. Preachers hesitate to express the gospel's awesome demands to congregations of the half-interested, escaping into jokey chat or explorations of social issues in secular terms, with occasional references to Jesus, just to add a few heavenly currants to the worldly pudding.

Some churches are more like social clubs than support groups for taking the converted forward in their journey from justification to holiness, so magnificently explored in Paul's letters and John Wesley's sermons. Sometimes keeping a church going is the main preoccupation of worshippers. In that respect a church may not be unlike a team playing in the bottom division of the football league.

While Manchester United, whose players earn more in a week than most people do in a year, attracts tens of thousands of supporters from all over the country and beyond, those at the foot of division three struggle to stay clear of the official receiver's grasp and, as one manager recently put it, have difficulty finding the cash when the players' boots need new laces. Some churches live in the no-money-for-laces world, and anxiety about that blunts the preacher's impact.

But let us not be deterred. In a deconverted world, the challenge to restore faith is no less exciting than was the challenge to convert when the Christian era was in its prime. By what other means than God's salvation plan may the problems of the new millennium be resolved? Their nature is powerfully encapsulated in the foreword to the *Oxford History of the Twentieth Century*:

> The twentieth century opened with a paradoxical combination of hope and fear. The hope rested on the expectation that the world was entering a new Golden Age and that such scientific discoveries and technological developments as electricity, the internal combustion engine, aeronautics, and advances in medical science would free humanity from all the sufferings – poverty, disease, famine, war – that had afflicted it since the beginning of recorded history. The fear arose from the apparent disintegration of traditional values and social structures, both secular and religious, that had bound society together in face of all those evils, and from the prospect that the world was therefore confronting a future in which only the strongest and most ruthless would survive.[1]

The fear expressed in the second part of that arresting analysis has proved to be fully justified. It has ever been the case that our increasing understanding of the workings of the world, and consequent mastery of its mechanisms and resources, has brought as many

problems as it has solved. Who has the answer to those
problems? The preacher, who brings God into the
situation; who evokes his living presence; who creates the
conditions for an encounter between him and those who
hear his word proclaimed.

Day after day, our newspapers and television screens
are filled with events to do with people's quest for wealth,
fame and power. We live in the era of the celebrity: the
man or woman whose possession of those things is
constantly depicted in the media and widely applauded.
Over against that, the preacher is chosen by God to be the
means by which he confronts, challenges and redeems his
creation.

When, in the present condition of Western society, we
preachers become disheartened in attempting to carry out
the awesome responsibility God has laid upon us, it is as
well to recall that occasional doubt and despondency have
been part of the preacher's inheritance down the centuries.
John Donne's faith was not always secure; John Wesley
had his moments of dark despair after Aldersgate; Martin
Luther King was overcome at times with a sense of failure.
But when John Keble looked despairingly upon the
condition of England in the nineteenth century, he saw
clearly that only by continuing to use all means to bring
God close to his people would his final triumph be
assured. In his great sermon at St Mary's, Oxford, in 1833,
Keble asked what a Christian should do in face of the fact
that the nation was becoming alienated from God. His
answer was that we should strive for 'a constant sense of
God's presence'.[2] It is in awakening hearers to God's
nearness that preachers perform their highest task.

In one of his poems, Robert Browning has a bishop
discussing the nature of faith after dinner with a friend.
The bishop speaks of how God has many ways of waking
our minds and senses to new discoveries about him:

Just when we are safest, there's a sunset touch,
A fancy from a flower-bell, someone's death,
A chorus from Euripides

And that's enough for fifty hopes and fears,
As old and new at once as Nature's self,
To rap and knock and enter in our soul.[3]

The preacher's rap and knock at the door of worshippers' minds and senses awakens them to the presence of God among them. The sermon is, in its beginning and its end, God's event. By its power, the *shekinah*, the glory of the one who is Alpha and Omega, is disclosed.

REFERENCES

Chapter 1

1. Ed. John Haggard, *Donne*, Nonesuch Press, London 1955, p.609.

2. Garrison Keillor, *Leaving Home*, Faber and Faber, London 1993, p.28.

3. Ed. Percy Livingstone Parker, *The Journal of John Wesley*, STL Productions, Bromley, p.307.

4. C B Firth, *From Napoleon to Hitler*, Ginn, London 1952, p.381.

5. Ed. Hugh Trevor-Roper, *Hitler's Table Talk*, Weidenfeld and Nicolson, London 1953, p.524.

6. H A L Fisher, *A History of Europe*, Eyre & Spottiswoode, London 1935, Preface.

7. Paul Scott Wilson, *The Practice of Preaching*, Abingdon Press, Nashville USA 1995, pp.22-24.

8. Peter Barber, 'What is the Focus of Worship?' *Local Preachers Magazine*, LPMA Sept. 1999.

Chapter 2

1. Ed. Ruth Gledhill, *The Times Book of Best Sermons*, Cassell, London 1995, Introduction.

2. Christopher Catherwood, *Martyn Lloyd-Jones: A Family Portrait*, Kingsway Publications, Eastbourne 1995, p.64.

3. *Sangster of Westminster*, Marshall, Morgan & Scott, London l960, p.79.

4. Christopher Catherwood, *The Best of Martyn Lloyd-Jones*, Baker Books, Grand Rapids USA l992, p.27.

5. Article by Anthony King in *The Daily Telegraph*, 3l December l999.

6. George Ade, *People You Know*, l903.

7. Ed. Leslie Houlden, *Austin Farrer: The Essential Sermons*, SPCK, London l99l, Introduction.

8. Speech in Bedford, 20 July l957.

9. Vance Packard, *The Hidden Persuaders*, Longmans Green, London l957.

10. Arthur Marwick, *The Sixties*, OUP l998.

11. Ed. Julian Hall, *Children's Rights*, Panther, London l972.

12. Neil Postman, *Teaching as a Subversive Activity*, Penguin Education Specials, Harmondsworth l971.

13. Arnold Shaw, *Sinatra*, Hodder Paperbacks, London l970, p.l2.

14. Alistair Cooke, *The Camel Driver and the Transistor*, British Association Guildhall Lectures, Granada Television, Manchester l965, p.43.

15. Blaise Pascal, *Lettres Provinciales*, l657.

16. Paul Sangster, *Doctor Sangster*, Epworth Press, London l962, p.278.

Chapter 3

1. David Puttnam, *Information in the Living Society*, RSA Journal August/September 1996.

2. John Stuart Mill, *Essay on Liberty*, Thinker's Library, Watts & Company, London 1948, p.11.

3. Ibid, p.19.

4. *The Times*, 15 April 1999.

5. Ed. Joe Aldred, *Preaching with Power*, Cassell, London 1998, p.59.

6. Letter of Horace Walpole, *Oxford Dictionary of Quotations*, OUP 1999, p.801.

7. T K Abbott, *Kant's Introduction to Logic*, Longmans Green, London 1885, p.1.

8. David Wilkinson, *God, the Big Bang and Stephen Hawking*, Monarch Publications, Crowborough 1996, p.28.

Chapter 4

1. Carl Sandberg, 'Personality' in *The Wheel*, Macmillan, London 1965.

2. Ed. Richard Crossman, *The God That Failed*, Bantam Books, New York 1952, p.13.

3. John Milton, *Doctrine and Discipline*, 1662.

4. Jacob Bronowski, *The Ascent of Man*, Book Club Associates by arrangement with the BBC, London 1976, p.19.

5. John Stacey, *Groundwork of Theology*, Epworth Press, London 1977, p.161.

6. *The Times*, 9 April 1999.

7. John Dryden, *Religio Lac*, 1680.

8. Ed. Peter Medway, *The Receiving End*, Penguin Education, Harmondsworth 1973, p.68.

9. Ed. Clayborne Carson & Peter Holloran, *A Knock at Midnight: The Great Sermons of Martin Luther King Jr*, Little, Brown & Co (UK), London 1999, p.79.

Chapter 5

1. Jean-Paul Sartre, *Nausea*, 1938.

2. Martin Bedford, *Thought for the Day*, BBC Radio 4.

3. Tr. Arthur Boyars and Simon Franklin, *The Face Behind The Face: New Poems by Yevgeny Yuvtushenko*, Marion Boyars Publishers, London 1979, p.10.

4. Bernhard Anderson, *The Living World of the Old Testament*, Longman Group, Harlow 1981, p.170 *et seq*.

5. Norman Wallwork, *Blackbirds and Budgerigars: A Critical History of Methodist Liturgical Dress 1786-1986*, Methodist Sacramental Fellowship, Keswick 1986, p.17.

Chapter 6

1. Rose Fitzgerald Kennedy, *Times to Remember*, Collins, London 1974, p.379.

2. Ed. John Haggard, *Donne*, Nonesuch Press, London 1955, p.616.

3. *The Times*, 25 June 1992, letter by the Reverend David Prior.

4. *The Times*, 29 July 1975, letter by Monja Danischewsky.

5. Newsletter of the National Association of Head Teachers, *The Challenge of Change*, Autumn 1972.

6. Francis Clifford, *The Naked Runner*, Hodder Paperback, London 1978, p.25.

7. *The Times*, 18 December 1971.

8. Ed. Clayborne Carson & Peter Holloran, *A Knock at Midnight: The Great Sermons of Martin Luther King Jr*, Little, Brown & Co (UK), London 1999, Introduction.

Chapter 7

1. Ed. Michael Howard and Wm Roger Louis, *The Oxford History of the Twentieth Century*, OUP 1998, Foreword.

2. John Keble, *National Apostasy*, Keble College Archives.

3. Robert Browning, 'Bishop Blougram's Apology', 1855.

The permission of the following to reprint copyright material is gratefully acknowledged:

Coretta Scott King for the extract from *The American Dream*, copyright 1961 by Martin Luther King Jr, copyright renewed 1989 by Coretta Scott King; Marion Boyars Publishers for the poem *Metamorphoses* by Yevgeny Yuvtushenko; Doubleday of New York for correspondence between President Kennedy and his mother quoted in *Times to Remember* by Rose Fitzgerald Kennedy; The Reverend David Prior for his letter to *The Times*; Oxford University Press for the passage from *The Oxford History of the Twentieth Century*. Thanks also to the Warden of Keble College, Oxford, for use of the college archives to research John Keble's sermon, *National Apostasy*.